Sandiego - California
Los Amigo -

How Venture Capitalists Make Investment Decisions

Research for Business Decisions, No. 53

Gunter Dufey, Series Editor

Professor of International Business and Finance
The University of Michigan

Other Titles in This Series

No. 45 *A Forecast for the Grocery Retailing Industry in the 1980s* — James L. Brock

No. 46 *Multinational Accounting: A Research Framework for the Eighties* — Frederick D. S. Choi, ed.

No. 47 *Valuation of Savings and Loan Associations* — Philip W. Glasgo

No. 48 *Commercial Bank Underwriting of Municipal Revenue Bonds* — Paul A. Leonard

No. 49 *Technological Innovation: The R & D Work Environment* — Augustus Abbey

No. 50 *Salesperson Motivation and Performance: A Predictive Model* — Nicholas Carlton Williamson

No. 51 *Stock Exchange Listings, Firm Value, and Market Efficiency* — Gary C. Sanger

No. 52 *An Empirical Investigation of Multibank Holding Company Performance* — Ronald L. Schillereff

How Venture Capitalists Make Investment Decisions

by
Christine Cope Pence

UMI RESEARCH PRESS
Ann Arbor, Michigan

Produced and distributed by
UMI Research Press
an imprint of
University Microfilms International
Ann Arbor, Michigan 48106

Library of Congress Cataloging in Publication Data

Pence, Christine Cope.
How venture capitalists make investment decisions.

(Research for business decisions ; no. 53)
"A revision of the author's thesis, University of California, Irvine, 1981"–T.p. verso.
Bibliography: p.
Includes index.
1. Venture capital. 2. Investments–Decision making.
I. Title. II. Series.

HG4963.P43 1982 658.1'52 82-8473
ISBN 0-8357-1362-8 AACR2

To Sheen and Steve
who, like the venture capitalists,
willingly gambled on the outcome of this project.

Contents

List of Tables

List of Figures

Acknowledgments

The perseverance, patience, and fortitude of the doctoral student is matched only by that of her dissertation chairman. Without the assistance of George Brown, my mentor, I would have had great difficulty pursuing a subject area as illusive as the venture capital market seemed when the study was first begun years ago. In addition to those venture capitalists directly involved in this study, many members of the venture capital community at large have influenced my ideas. Notable among these was Walter Stults from NASBIC. Another was Bob Rawlins whose wise, experienced counsel helped bring into focus the relevant topics in venture proposals. Beyond the assistance provided by the venture capital community, and the encouragement and support given by my fellow students, especially David Krackhardt, must be mentioned.

All finished works reach that stage because someone takes the time to edit them carefully for clarity, consistency, and readibility. Connie Barrowman spent many hours helping me with this process. The final editing and typing was handled efficiently by Barbara McAlpine, whose professionalism made the final stages of the production reasonably painless.

The last but most enduring of the contributors to the creation and completion of this paper was Jane Pence, my mother, who continues to support me psychologically in all my endeavors.

To all of these people I have mentioned directly, and to the countless others I have neglected to mention—thank you.

Christine Cope Pence
Fall 1980

1

Introduction

You're not really going to invest all that money solely on gut reaction, are you?

Over the years, the American economy has continued to expand due in part to the contribution made by new businesses in terms of stimulation of technological innovation. The cycle of new business formation and eventual absorption into the mainstream of economic activity generates new jobs which result in increased personal spending ability.[1]

An integral part of any enterprise's continuing economic success is its ability first to obtain appropriate financing at critical points in its development, and then to manage those funds efficiently and effectively. Each stage in the economic growth of an enterprise is associated with different financial needs. As the enterprise grows in size and ability to sustain itself in its marketplace, alternative sources of financing become available which, if used efficiently, will permit the enterprise to continue its growth.

While the problems associated with established enterprises of any size are important, the problems associated with a new enterprise and its ability to obtain financing are the most critical to the perpetuation of the American economic system as it has evolved over the past two hundred years. The American economic system depends upon the creation of new technologies which become assimilated into the marketplace through new enterprises. These new enterprises then grow into larger enterprises which in turn spin off another generation of new enterprises. Although there are exceptions to this pattern of assimilating new technologies into the marketplace, the important factor is that new technologies do get to the marketplace. The marketplace then expands through the introduction of new technologies and new enterprises.

Because the financial community plays such a critical role in the new enterprise's development, it is important both to identify the economic factors which affect decision-making and to understand the relationship between the relevant economic factors and the ultimate investment decision.

Much interest has been focused lately on the issues surrounding availability of capital and credit for the new business. Generally, the assumption made is that both capital and credit are difficult to obtain for the new business. Little attention has been given to the basic economic factors which affect the availability of such capital and credit. In order to suggest corrections for improving the flow of capital and credit, first it must be established which factors affect that flow. These factors potentially might be classified in two categories: those external to the new enterprise which include the marketplace at large, and those internal to the firm which include its internal mechanics.

There exists a specialized community of investors called venture capitalists, which supports the financial needs of the new, technologically-oriented enterprise through all the critical points in the enterprise's development. Of particular interest here is that early stage of development when little proven history exists. It is at this point in the enterprise's formation that the inherent risks to the investor can be the greatest and yet the potential returns the highest. Generally, venture capitalists invest in small businesses which intend to become large either in their field or in the marketplace as a whole. The larger the enterprise becomes, the greater the potential return to the original investor.

Entrepreneurial activity drives the economic mechanism which results in new business formation and ultimate assimilation into the mainstream marketplace. The following chart illustrates the sequence relationships between entrepreneurial activity, small business, and large business.

Figure 1. Typical Sequence of Activity

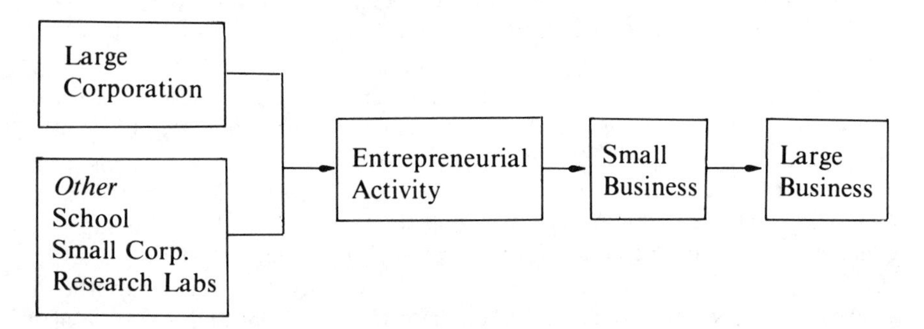

Entrepreneurs who choose to start their own business primarily come out of existing companies which they either started or worked for as an employee. In the first case, these entrepreneurs will have some form of track record of their ability to start a viable operation. In the latter case, these individuals will have come from two types of situations: (1) relatively small and new companies or (2) established, relatively large companies. Those from the small, new companies come to the newest enterprise with some history of how to keep a small, new company operating and moving toward larger market shares. Those from established older companies come either with proven management ability and a desire to try it on their own, or with a product idea which they feel they can market and for a variety of reasons prefer to do so through their own company. A third pool of entrepreneurs exists in academic institutions, primarily in the scientific-oriented research programs; a fourth group may be found in research laboratories outside of the academic community. No matter the working history of these individuals, they all share a sense of rugged individualism and need to obtain the American ideal of pursuing a new frontier in terms of a new company.

During the entrepreneurial activity phase, prototype products are developed. At some point during the development of this prototype, a new business is formed, frequently in a garage shop. The next few years of high growth by this new business should bring it to the size of a large business in terms of employees (over 1,000) and total sales (in excess of $20 million). At this point, the entrepreneurial process recycles.

One of the keys which keeps this process recycling is the capital market. Basically, the capital market supplies funds from lenders to entrepreneurs who in turn recycle funds back to the lenders.

Figure 2. The Capital Market

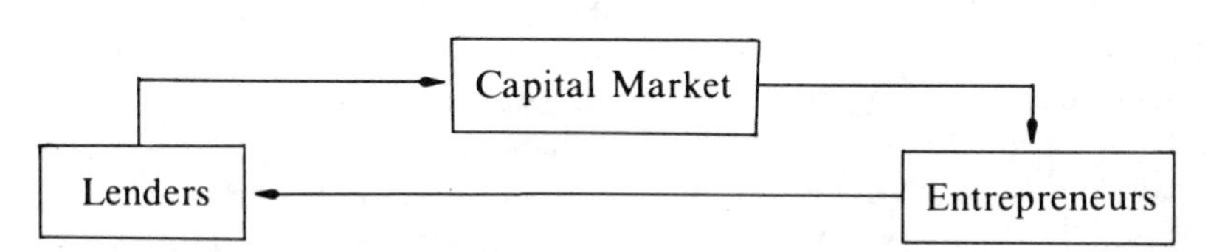

There are four basic categories of lenders in this particular capital market: individuals (who also can be venture capitalists); government (e.g., FHA, SBA); institutions (banks, SBICs, venture firms, secured lenders, corporations); public markets. Each of these lenders has a particular function in the financial future of the new enterprise. The growth cycle of the new business can be described in terms of the critical points for additional capital investment: (1) seed/start-up, (2) start-up with prototype developed, (3) growth/expansion, (4) bridge (for public market), (5) buy out. Traditionally, the first stage is covered by the individual investor. The second stage is financed primarily by individuals, government agencies, and venture capital institutions. The later stages traditionally have been financed by the institutions as well. It should be noted that these financings at the later stages of development primarily are arranged through the use of debt instruments, while earlier stage financings are done with a combination of debt and equity.

The factors which affect the availability of credit and venture capital fall into three categories: economic climate; perceived risk-reward ratios; exit opportunities. The economic climate appears to affect both the availability of funds/credit for new business and the quality/quantity of new businesses that seek such funds/credit. This classic chicken and egg problem results in the following general relationship. As the economic climate improves throughout the economy, more venture capitalists are willing to invest in new businesses; more banks have funds which they are willing to lend; more banks seek new business and are willing to extend new lines of credit with somewhat lower interest rates. With regard to new business formation during improving economic conditions, it appears that a greater quantity and quality of entrepreneurs emerge from both the large corporation and the smaller enterprise into the mainstream of new business activity. The reverse relationships in terms of availability of funds/credit and qualified numbers of entrepreneurs appear when economic conditions are declining.

The second factor, perceived risk-reward ratios, is closely tied to the economic climate. Financiers will fund new business only if they can make sufficient after-tax-returns on their investment. The greater the perceived risk involved, the less likely will be the availability of credit. On the other hand, venture funds will be available for increasingly risky deals. Elaborate financial structuring schemes which serve to mitigate risk in the venture capitalist's mind often are closely related with riskier deals. In these situations, the combination of such terms as negative covenants, preferred stock, and convertible debentures can be expected. On the other hand, other venture capitalists prefer to have increasingly less elaborate structuring schemes as the perceived risk increases. In these situations, it can be expected that the financier desires only common stock for his cash investment. However the venture capitalist mitigates the risk, it is clear that each financier has a threshold of perceived risk-to-return above which he will not make the investment.

The third factor, exit opportunities, again is closely tied with economic conditions and perceived risk-reward ratios. Worsening economic conditions can affect the business's ability to survive. Financiers extending credit expect that the new enterprise will need to use lines of credit, but will be unable in the near future to repay the necessary funds. The financier, therefore, will survive existing accounts rather than extend new credit lines to new accounts.

For the venture capitalist, exit opportunities constitute just one of many variables to be considered when determining perceived risk-reward ratios. Because this analysis involves a decision which usually will be made at least five years downstream, the current economic climate does not directly affect the decision to invest in terms of exit opportunities. However, the current economic climate does suggest the general direction of the economy, which in turn indicates the likelihood the new enterprise will be able to succeed. With that success, the financier will be in a position to exit the investment by whatever available means will maximize the investor's return on investment.

This paper focuses primarily on the broad economic question of what factors tend to encourage (discourage) lenders to support entrepreneurial activity in the early phase of a business's life cycle. The lenders' (venture capitalists) decisions are made in an environment of uncertainty since little operating history exists for extensive analysis of the new firm, and hence a large amount of risk of capital loss is associated with the decision. Earlier, it was suggested that these factors might be categorized as those which are external to the new enterprise comprised by the marketplace, and those which are internal to the new enterprise and represent functional areas of operation. Since theoretically it appears that the state of the general economic climate will affect a potential investor's financial decisions concerning the new enterprise, it is important to establish this study in its relevant economic climate.

The study itself consisted of two phases: an initial phase during which the venture capitalists formulated opinions on a set of three potential venture projects; and a follow-up phase in which the researcher conducted intensive interviews with the venture capitalists concerning their investment decision for each of the three venture projects presented. The three venture projects were mailed to the selected venture capitalists in December of 1978 and the first part of January 1979. Interviews were conducted from January 2, 1979 through March 14, 1979.

Most of the fourth quarter 1978 statistics publicly were available to the venture capital community as background information on the state of the economy, if they chose to use them. Using some set of information, they were able to develop an opinion on the prevailing economic climate which, in some way, might have influenced their investment decision.

While some economists were predicting that a recessionary trend was beginning in the fourth quarter of 1978, most economists found the indicators to be illustrating the confusion within the marketplace, where no decisive statement could be made regarding the general economic climate and its future.

Real GNP for the fourth quarter 1978 increased at a seasonally adjusted annual rate of 6.9% over the previous quarter ($1391.4 billion in the third quarter to $1414.7 billion in the fourth quarter).[2] GNP prices as measured by the fixed-weighted price index increased at an annual rate of 8.4%. The implicit price deflator, which reflects price changes as well as shifts in the composition of goods and services that make up GNP, increased 8.2%. Personal consumption expenditures increased 7.1%, primarily due to the large increases in energy expenditures of 10.9% and food expenditures of 7.7%. Prices paid by government and investors combined increased 10%.

Unemployment during the fourth quarter 1978 declined from 6% to 5.8% which resulted in an employment-population ratio of 59.0% for the fourth quarter. Interestingly, the largest increases in employment continued to be in manufacturing (primarily durable goods), distributive operations (transportation and public utilities, and wholesale/retail trade), and services (services, finance, insurance, and real estate). Average weekly hours in the private nonfarm economy were up over the third quarter to 35.9 from 35.8. Manufacturing industry hours increased from 40.4 to 40.6.

Personal income continued to increase in the fourth quarter to an annual rate of $57.3 billion. Wages and salaries increased at an annual rate of $36.2 billion. Personal taxes increased at an annual rate of $11.9 billion. Real disposable personal income increased 5.2% in the fourth quarter. Saving as a percent of disposable personal income increased 4.8%. Personal consumption expenditures increased 7.6%.

Real nonresidential fixed investment increased 9.5%, due in large part to the increases in structures and producers' durable equipment. Residential investment also increased by 4%. Housing starts averaged $2.08 million (seasonally adjusted annual rate).

Total private liquid asset holdings for nonfinancial investors increased 3% in the fourth quarter. While holdings in time deposits, short term marketable securities, and negotiable certificates of deposit all increased between 3% and 4%, investments in other private money market instruments increased 12%. The Federal Reserve's policy of controlling inflation by increasing the discount rate (8–9.5%) may have caused all of this increase in investment in private money market instruments. The change in the discount rate led directly to an increase in the prime rate (9.75% to 11.75%) charged by banks. Net change in the amount of consumer installment credit outstanding was up 10% even though figures were seasonally adjusted. While bank loans and investments continued to grow in the fourth quarter, it was at a more gradual rate than the previous quarter (2%).

Business inventory-sales ratio fell slightly in the fourth quarter (1.39); however, total business inventories and sales continued to rise to a high at year end of $273,776 million in sales and $379,391 million in inventories (both seasonally adjusted). Manufacturers' inventory to shipment ratio declined 3% during the fourth quarter from 1.53 to 1.48, though both total shipments and inventories rose (shipments 5%; inventories 2%). Manufacturers' new orders increased 8% primarily due to an 11% increase in durable goods; however, manufacturers' unfilled orders also increased by 7%.

During the middle of the fourth quarter of 1978, the stock markets suffered a setback from the previous quarter, but had begun to recover by December. The Dow-Jones industrial average closed out the year at 807.94; the composite index for all the stocks on the New York Stock Exchange was at 53.69. Dividend-price ratio for common stock yields was 5.39%; earnings-price ratio was 12.85%, which was up from 11.32% for the previous quarter.

The overall picture, then, was of an economy in a reasonably sound position which was not facing change imminently. One major uncertainty was the ultimate impact and timing of a reduced national income due to the effects of changes in the Federal Revenue Act of 1978 and of local property tax law changes passed in California and New York in 1978.

The Federal Revenue Act of 1978 cut effective tax rates for individuals, increased the standard deduction, and increased personal exemptions. In addition to the changes for individuals, the Act reduced corporation tax rates (reducing the maximum rate from 48% to 46%), reduced corporate capital gains from 30% to 28%, and liberalized the investment credit. The California and New York legislation reduced property taxes.

The interviews for this study were conducted essentially during the first quarter of 1979. The previous quarter had been reasonably satisfactory. Economists were forecasting a recession, but no one felt the economy would change dramatically. In retrospect, it is interesting to note what did occur economically during the first quarter of 1979. The venture capitalists were being interviewed during this quarter and may have used current information in making their current investment decisions.

Real GNP did slow its growth in the first quarter to an annual rate of increase of .5% after the 7% increase experienced in the last quarter of 1978. This slow-down was due in large measure to the harsh winter weather conditions prevailing throughout the country for most of the quarter. The activities predominantly affected were those associated with construction.

GNP prices (measured by the fixed-weight price index) increased at an annual rate of 9.5%, while the GNP implicit price deflator increased 8.7%. Prices of personal consumption expenditures increased 10.5% on an annual basis as a result of increases in energy (17%) and food (19%). Prices paid by government and investors combined increased 8%, annual rate.

Unemployment again was reduced, this time to a rate of 5.7%. The total labor force continued to increase by 950,000, with an employment-population ratio of 59.4%. Employment increased mostly in manufacturing (especially durables) and trades. Transportation equipment and electrical/non-electrical machinery showed the sharpest increases.

Personal income increased at an annual rate of $45 billion; wages and salaries increased $35.5 billion at an annual rate. The legislative changes regarding personal income taxes from 1978 resulted in a decline of $4.5 billion in personal taxes on an annual basis. In California and New York, first quarter state and local tax payments were reduced by $3 billion. Disposable personal income continued to increase by $49.5 billion, annual rate. Given the increase in prices, the resulting real disposable personal income only increased 3%.

Real personal consumption expenditures increased slightly, up 1.5% at an annual rate. Expenditures on services increased 5.5%, while goods declined.

Real nonresidential fixed investment increased only slightly, up 2.5% at an annual rate, mostly due to a decline in construction. This decline in construction primarily was a result of the inclement weather conditions. Expenditures for producers' durable equipment increased 8%.

Real residential investment declined 14%, annual rate, primarily as a result of the weather. Housing starts dropped to 1.68 million in January, 1.38 million in February, and increased to 1.79 million in March. Also affecting housing starts was the increasing mortgage interest rate which was reflected in the discount rate of 9.5 at the end of March and the prime rate of 11.75 for the same period. Demand for loans dropped. The spread between the prime rate and the rate on mortgages may partly explain the move for banks to make loans to business.

Real inventory investment increased to $12 billion, annual rate, with most of the investment in durable manufacturing. The rate of investment remained relatively the same as in the fourth quarter of 1978. Business sales declined slightly, resulting in an inventory-sales ratio of 1.41. Manufacturers' new orders increased slightly, while manufacturers' unfilled orders continued to increase by 7%. Manufacturers' inventory-shipments ratio increased slightly, indicating that a trend in inventory investment might be beginning.

On the stock exchanges, the Dow-Jones industrial average continued to increase, closing March at 847.84. The Standard and Poor's composite index closed at 100.11, and the New York Stock Exchange composite index closed at 56.19. The dividend-price ratio dropped slightly by the end of March to 5.36 as opposed to 5.39 at the end of December 1978.

By the end of March, private liquid asset holdings of nonfinancial investors were up to $1,792.1 billion, seasonally adjusted; an increase of 2% over the previous quarter. An 8% increase in investment in short term marketable securities and a 10% increase in investments in other private money market instruments were the most interesting of notable shifts in liquid asset investments.

Again, the economic picture at the end of the first quarter still did not indicate clearly an imminent recession. While signals were beginning to emerge, such as the increase in unfilled orders and the slight increase in liquid holdings of nonfinancial investors, none of the signals were indicative of a recession within the next quarter. The change in tax laws did have an effect, which could not be measured in its entirety at that time. Corporate profit figures were not available, though there appeared to be a slight downward trend. However, with the impact of new tax legislation, the final picture of corporate profit change might not have been as dramatic. As the money markets began to offer higher returns, it appeared that the marketplace responded favorably by shifting liquid assets from time and demand deposits into other private money-market instruments.

Given the economic setting from December 1978 through March 1979, this research project was designed to determine which factors really affect the investment decision for venture capitalists who invest in early-stage innovative companies. Thirty-five venture capitalists participated in the study in which they analyzed three hypothetical investment proposals. Additionally, they participated in an intensive interview with the researcher during which they discussed their analysis of the proposals.

Chapter 2 of this paper presents a theoretical basis for the study, both from the perspective of the available literature on small business investment by venture capitalists, and from the perspective of relevant financial analytical techniques. Since no known precedent exists for the approach taken in analyzing this research question, the choice of relevant theoretical literature was made on the basis of which body of knowledge helped define the void and which body of knowledge provided the analytical financial foundation from which to study the void.

In Chapter 3, the methodology used for the project is discussed. In particular, the questions which the project intended to illuminate are detailed. The experimental design of the project is explained, followed by a discussion of the research documents which were used as tools for eliciting the venture capitalists' investment rationale. These documents are the three venture proposals which were designed specifically for this purpose.

Chapter 4 presents the results of the study. A demographic discussion of the sample of venture capitalists and justifications for their selection is presented. The approach for reducing the data from a qualitative to a quantitative form is explained, followed by detailed data analysis.

Chapter 5 summarizes this particular study in terms of its contribution to the knowledge base. A discussion of improvements in the technique and refinements in the research document follows. The chapter concludes with a statement of what still remains to be explored through future research projects.

Participating Venture Capital Organizations

Abbot Capital Corporation
Allied Capital Corporation
Asset Management Company
BankAmerica Capital Corporation
Bessemer Securities Corporation
Brentwood Associates
California Northwest Fund, Inc.
The Charles River Partnership
Community Investment Enterprises, Inc.
Continental-Illinois Venture Corporation
Control Data Capital Corporation
Federal Street Capital Corporation
Fidelity Venture Associates, Inc.
First Capital Corporation of Chicago and
First Chicago Investment Corporation
First Midwest Capital Corporation
First Venture Capital Corporation of Boston
Hambrecht and Quist
Idanta Partners
Institutional Venture Associates
Inverness Capital Corporation
Kleiner, Perkins, Caufield, & Byers
Donald L. Lucas
Mayfield II
Morgenthaler Associates
New Court Securities Corporation
Northwest Growth Fund, Inc.
The Palmer Organization
Research and Science Investors, Inc.
Sutter Hill Ventures
T.A. Associates
Union Venture Corporation
UST Capital Corporation
Welsh, Carson, Anderson, and Stowe
Westland Capital Corporation
WestVan

2

Literature Review

There have been two primary tacks taken in studying the issues which affect financing of new, innovative enterprises. The first approach essentially focused on predicting a venture capitalist's success/failure rate in a portfolio design theory context. The second approach has attempted to establish the existence of a real need for venture capital and credit for the young enterprise in order to support federal legislative proposals.

In his dissertation of 1976,[1] Hoban attempted first to identify a set of universal characteristics of venture capital investments which could be reduced to a predictive set of variables. This predictive set then could be used to determine the ultimate success or failure of an enterprise contained in the venture capitalist's portfolio. While the approach taken to the problem of predicting portfolio success was novel, in the long-run, factors which led to the issue of risk could not be reduced to a single scale. Such problems as the individuality and uniqueness of each portfolio investment prohibited the creation of a constant set of predictive variables across all venture investments. Other risk factors such as economic conditions, market conditions, and entrepreneurial ability also did not fit easily into a single scale.

In Poindexter's 1976 dissertation,[2] an attempt was made to measure the amount of risk venture capital investors assume as a first step in determining the efficiency of the marketplace. In this case, the instrument used to determine marketplace efficiency was the Capital Asset Pricing Model. The results showed that this particular model was an inadequate predictor of market risk differentials for the venture capital market. Here again, one of the problems arose out of the lack of a common definition for venture capital market risk. It is not entirely clear that definitions of market risk in other capital markets fully explain the market risk in the venture capital market.

A dissertation by Wells in 1974[3] addressed the issue of risk and reward within the venture capitalist's portfolio. This descriptive field study of seven venture capital firms attempted to analyze perceived risk-reward trade-offs in terms of operating risk, man-time risk, and stock market risk. While this was a first attempt at describing perceived risk-reward trade-offs, difficulties arose in establishing common definitions of risk which universally characterized all portfolio investments. Wells concluded that venture capitalists were indeed risk-averse, assuming that their expectations of returns reflected the actual returns made.

The second approach used in studying the issues which affect financing of new, innovative businesses primarily involved the establishment of a need for equity financing as a justification for designing and implementing public policy. There have been many studies in the last few years which address various facets of the "equity gap" issue. One of the early studies was conducted by Charles River Associates for the ETIP program (Experimental Technology Incentive Program).[4] This study examined the structure of the venture capital industry in order to determine the extent of internal market imperfections. While the study concluded that no such imperfections existed, it also noted that based on a study of publicly-held venture capital firms and SBICs, it could not support the argument that venture capitalists made inordinately high average returns.

Shortly after the CRA study, several studies emerged from various government agencies which approached the "equity gap" issue from the perspective that the gap did exist and that public policy should be redesigned which would not interfere with the efficient operation of the venture capital market. Typical of this approach was the National Bureau of Standards ETIP program report which was jointly sponsored with the U.S. Securities and Exchange Commission.[5] This particular report outlined the SEC rules and regulations which affected the allocation of funds to new businesses. The ETIP program ultimately was to design a monitoring system whereby the effects of SEC regulation on the flow of venture capital funds to new enterprises could be observed.

With the blossoming of the Office of the Chief Counsel for Advocacy, U.S. Small Business Administration, under the guidance of Milton Stewart since 1978, has come a renewed interest in conducting economic research which will lead to a sound understanding of all the economic issues surrounding small business. While most of the work regarding venture capital and credit availability to date has been of a descriptive nature,[6] the SBA's interest has spurred several government agencies to evaluate the issues. One of the more complete descriptive studies was undertaken by Cohen for the Federal Reserve.[7]

Since 1978, there have been innumerable legislative hearings conducted on capital formation and the effects of government regulation on the efficient allocation of capital to new businesses.[8] Again, most of the testimony has been of a descriptive nature, and therefore not conducive to quantitative evaluation.

Given this general body of background literature on the venture capital market and technical approaches to studying the market, it becomes necessary to define more carefully this particular study and the technical body of research used to justify this approach. While, in the long run, portfolio analysis may prove to be a useful tool for evaluating venture capital investments, most researchers heretofore have concluded that the direct application of existing theory falls apart because of the definitions used for risk and return. The sheer number of potentially relevant variables which may comprise an appropriate definition for venture investments has caused most researchers to avoid the issue. Because intellectually the universe of potential variables seemed to differ by stage of investment, this researcher chose to reduce the universe of instruments to be analyzed. Only first-stage financings, those involving early-stage, start-up companies were considered. In addition, only technologically innovative companies were of direct interest to the researcher.

In the summer of 1978, a preliminary series of interviews with venture capitalists across the country was conducted. The goal of these interviews was to become familiar with issues with which the practicing investment community was concerned. Out of those interviews came the awareness that no matter the investing company, nor the potential investment candidate, three basic categories of variables affected the ultimate investment decision: (1) the potential investment candidate as a business; (2) the economic environment in which the investment decision was being made; (3) the demographics of the investing firm, including its portfolio design philosophy and current investment position. When evaluated by the venture capitalist, some intricate combination of variables within each of the categories and across all the categories was used to make the ultimate investment decision. This study was designed to identify a set of relevant decision variables.

While the investment decision is made using some combination of variables across the aforementioned categories of variables, three investment criteria traditionally are used in financial investment decisions regardless of the investment: (1) return on investment; (2) risk; (3) liquidity. Traditional academic financial literature treats these three criteria in the context of the large firm or at least a firm which has some existing history for analysis. While a context of decision-making under uncertainty has been superimposed on these theoretical discussions of large firms, the environment still involves only the later-stage enterprises and not the start-up enterprise.

However, this body of theory is all that is available presently for evaluating the decision-making process of venture capitalists. By focusing on start-up, technologically innovative enterprises some formal definitions must be altered in order to incorporate those facets involving uncertainty which differ from the context of an established enterprise.

The ultimate long range goal of a venture capital firm is wealth-maximization. Wealth maximization results from a number of factors which venture capitalists emphasize in different proportions: (1) long term returns on invested capital; (2) short term returns on invested capital; (3) management assistance programs; (4) community educational programs; (5) other indirect income-producing activities such as community involvement. Invested capital can cover a range of investments from purely venture to various types of money market instruments. Obviously, the investment decision involves both the issue of portfolio balance and of the desirability of the individual investment regardless of its potential role in the portfolio.

Concentrating for the moment on the potential individual investment as it relates to the investment decision, it becomes evident why the type of investment determines a unique strategy for investment analysis. An investment in a firm with several years of history lends itself to a more certain estimate of the potential return than does an investment in a firm with little historical data. Addressing strictly those potential investments which involve new, technologically innovative firms, financial literature implies that an evaluation of return, risk, and liquidity will determine the investment decision, if the investor is rational.

It is difficult to speak of return separately from risk. One would expect that as risk increases, potential return also should increase, providing the investment has validity and credibility. While liquidity as a function of the investment decision is tied to return and risk, it can be separated from the other two more readily.

Available capital budgeting techniques suggest that if the decision environment is one of certainty, then the evaluation of an investment using the Net Present Value Method or perhaps the Internal Rate of Return Method should lead to the appropriate decision. However, the investment decision defined in this study definitely involves uncertainty. Some criterion must be utilized whereby both return and risk are evaluated. Techniques such as Risk-Adjusted Discount Rates and Certainty Equivalents change the Net Present Value Method of valuation to include risk, in the latter case by adjusting the numerator of the equation, and in the former case by adjusting the denominator.[9]

In evaluating new businesses, determining the value of R (return on investment or net cash flow), not to mention the value of k (marginal cost of capital or discount rate), requires great psychic ability. In most cases, just determining an appropriate riskless return is impossible. However, in some manner, venture capitalists do determine an expected value for investments, given the existence of overwhelming uncertainty. Their accuracy in determining these expected cash flows will be left for another study. Suffice it to say now that those who continue to invest in these new, technologically innovative businesses appear to be satisfied with their results enough to continue making investments of this type.

Liquidity as a criterion of the venture capitalist's investment decision means ability to convert a cash investment back into cash for reinvestment.

Again, liquidity can be discussed in terms of a portfolio criterion or a singular investment criterion. As a portfolio criterion, the issue can become one of ability to meet maturing obligations. However, in the typical venture capital portfolio, aside from ones which borrow extensively from the Small Business Administrations (SBICs), the issue of meeting debt obligations makes little sense. Instead, depending upon their organizational structure, venture capital firms are more concerned with one or both of the following issues: (1) ability to convert investments to cash or near equivalents at the maximum value in order to liquidate the venture capital organization's agreement; (2) ability to convert to cash in order to reinvest in either existing portfolio investments or in new activities.

Liquidity in terms of an individual investment means ability to convert the original cash investment back to cash. Several factors are involved in evaluating convertibility ease, not the least of which is the establishment of a market value for the investment candidate. Again, the issues of risk and return on investment tangle with the issue of liquidity in the sense that determining ultimate potential for liquidity involves the determination of the length of time that will be necessary to reach a desired return. The evaluation involves the establishing of a marketplace for the new company so that the marketplace can determine its value by setting a price for the company and/or its stock. Obviously, the marketplace will be evaluating, among other criteria, the liquidity position of the new company in the traditional sense of current and quick ratios. However, the venture capitalist's definition of liquidity more directly involves the ability of the venture firm to sell out its position in the new business. Formal financial theory provides little assistance in evaluating the liquidity criterion from the venture capitalist's perspective beyond what is offered indirectly through the Certainty-Equivalent Adjusted-Net-Present-Value Method discussed earlier.

Turning to the venture capitalist's overall portfolio, financial theory offers several approaches, of which four stand out as potentially being useful: (1) Chance-Constrained Programming Model, (2) Long-Run Growth Model, (3) Expected Utility Models, (4) Mean-Variance Models. The Poindexter dissertation[10] mentioned earlier attempted one such application of the Capital Asset Pricing Model (a mean-variance model), but found it ineffective in explaining venture capital portfolio management. No known further work has been conducted in the area of portfolio design which deals specifically with venture capitalists' portfolios. It is likely that this lack of extension of theoretical portfolio design is due in part to the difficulty in clearly defining the relevant risk characteristics of investments in new, technologically innovative enterprises. Without a public marketplace evaluation of the investment's worth in terms of daily quotes for the stock, it becomes difficult to discuss the investment in terms of Beta values as would be required by the mean-variance models. The difficulties associated with applying the expected utility models under most practical situations make them an even less attractive approach for characterizing portfolio design in this case. However, over time this approach may prove to be effective, assuming utilities can be determined for venture investors. Chance-constrained programming models suggest the objective should be to maximize expected return on the portfolio, subject to maintaining a minimum return. It may prove useful in explaining how venture capitalists design their portfolios. The Long-Run Growth Model again focuses on the "how-to" problem rather than on what actually is being done.

The issue, then, primarily is one of finding an appropriate model which will describe and explain what is being done by the practicing community rather than of establishing normative models which might be used by this community. At this point in theoretical development, the venture capital portfolio has yet to be described accurately across the myriad of types of investors who participate in venture capital investments. The inherent risks of this type of investment have yet to be fully exposed or quantitatively evaluated. This particular study attempts to add to the understanding of the factors which the investment community considers to be relevant in determining their investment decision. It does not attempt to develop theory which will predict better investment behavior from a portfolio design perspective.

3

Methodology

Why do venture capitalists choose to make some investments and not others? What criteria do they use to evaluate one prospective investment over another? In interviewing the venture community in the summer of 1978, frequently the response given was that they made an investment because they had a gut reaction about the deal, the product, or the people. Inherent in this statement is some method by which they evaluate the three financial criteria used to make financial decisions—risk, return on investment, and liquidity.

This study focuses strictly on that class of investments which includes new, technologically innovative enterprises. This particular group of investments involves businesses which have little substantive financial history appropriate for quantitative evaluation. As such, the potential risks are extremely great. Investments of this type often are likened to the games of chance played in Las Vegas; however, there is a distinct difference between the investor and the speculator. Investors are those who carefully study the risks of a potential investment, making the investment decision only when a reasonable margin of safety exists. This margin of safety may be based on the historical soundness of the enterprise itself. Speculators, on the other hand, invest on others' future expectations. These expectations often are justified by the excitement of the marketplace itself and not generally by the inherent soundness of the prospective candidate's business plan. In other words, the speculator justifies the investment based on the general investment climate, while the investor justifies the investment based on the strength of the business itself. This paper focuses on the investor.

A decision to commit funds to any one particular enterprise is likely to be made in the context of the investor's entire portfolio. If venture capitalists as a whole are rational investors, it can be assumed that they evaluate potential investment candidates based on the investment's merits as well as in terms of the investor's current portfolio needs. A common set of factors which is evaluated by all investors for all potential investments in new, technologically innovative enterprises does exist. It is expected, though, that different degrees of significance are placed on different aspects of any potential investment candidate. The problem, then, is to identify components of this common set of factors.

Many venture capitalists have stated that out of the several hundred prospective investments which cross their desks in a year, fewer than ten pass through the initial screening. Of the handful which pass through that initial screening, no more than two ultimately will receive financing by them.[1] Usually, only one will be financed by them. It is unknown how many of the rejected investment candidates eventually will receive financing by other venture capitalists or by other capital sources. What factors do the venture capitalists evaluate which justify the drastic reduction of prospective investments to two or fewer?

In order to begin to answer this question more precisely than the venture capitalists had with their "gut reaction" response, it was decided that an instrument must be designed which used the language of venture capitalists. This instrument had to be written in such a way that it would help elicit more perceptive responses than mere gut reaction. Obviously, gut reaction had to include many factors, not the least of which would be the educational benefits of having done it—the learning curve effect. Since a prospectus or business plan is demanded by most venture capitalists as the document most representative of the overall picture of an enterprise, it was decided that such a document would be a useful tool for eliciting the desired information. Since so few business plans make it past the initial screening, designing a plan which would be acceptable to most venture capitalists without knowing exactly which factors make a plan acceptable became a real challenge. Theoretically, it would have been possible to use a prospectus which had previously obtained financing; however, what one investor considers acceptable might not be universally acceptable. A case in point is the Amdahl financing. Although this was a later-stage investment in some respects, it was passed around to several members of the venture community who refused the opportunity to invest.[2] Ultimately, it received funding primarily from foreign investors. There are examples of early-stage investments which were turned down by some investors, however. One such example of an early-stage investment which ultimately received financing is Collagen, a medical products company based in the San Francisco Bay Area.

In order to write a business plan which would pass the initial screening of a majority of the investors, the scope of potential investments had to be reduced and clearly defined. Defining an appropriate plan always came back to the basic problem encountered in defining venture capital. Implying that venture capital was synonymous with risk capital meant that all types and stages of investment were potential candidates. It was felt that the most risky investment was one for which little substantiable evidence existed, and hence was the type of investment which was considered most appropriate for this study. It seemed that closely tied to general business risk was the notion of innovation. "Mom and Pop" grocery stores, while potentially risky investments, could be compared with similar businesses. These similar businesses would have historical evidence of their viability as enterprises, and could, in a sense, be used as comparison for measuring potential success of similar new businesses. Innovation, by definition, implies something new which has not been done before and therefore cannot be compared quite so directly with existing or former businesses. The conclusion, then, was that only those plans which involved new, innovative businesses would be considered for this study.

"Innovative" still did not narrow the field of potential business plans significantly. The other element of venture capital investments which seemed to be universally popular was a technological improvement or advancement. Technology can be defined in many ways; however, for this study, the relevant definition meant industrial, scientific, and marketing improvement. The appropriate field of consideration for creating a business plan thus had been narrowed to include only new, technologically innovative companies.

The last element remaining in this clarification of the appropriate business plan was that of the ultimate marketplace to which the new business was appealing. It was felt that two general marketplaces could be identified: (1) the industrial-service marketplace, and (2) the consumer marketplace. The industrial-service marketplace includes other technologically-oriented enterprises and service businesses such as specialized medical practices. The consumer marketplace includes all domestic consumers. While other marketplaces can be defined, it was felt that these two broad categories would cover those marketplace participants who would be interested in a product from a new, technologically innovative firm.

The odds were against designing a single business plan which would appeal to a large number of venture capitalists. It was decided, therefore, that three different plans should be designed in order to increase the likelihood of having at least one plan which would be of interest to any particular venture capitalist. Further, it was decided that these three plans should be representative of three different types of technological innovation. The first plan takes an existing technology from an industrial setting and translates it into a consumer product. The second plan takes an existing technological product and mass markets it innovatively. The third plan develops a whole new technology and then moves the resulting product from the research environment to the marketplace.

In reviewing several business plans which had received venture financing, several categories of information appeared repeatedly:

1. Summary of the plan and financing needs.
2. Description of the product(s).
3. Description of the marketplace environment including a discussion of the competition.

4. An outline of the organizational structure with resumes of key individuals on the management team.
5. A descriptive history of the firm.
6. A detailed statement of the firm's plan for meeting its stated goals and objectives (marketing and production plans).
7. Financial statements and projections.
8. Statement of the potential return for the investor including a discussion of foreseeable exit opportunities.

The plans to be used for this research study would have to include a similar set of information in some degree of detail, if they were to be considered representative of a typical plan.

As a first cut in determining what factors venture capitalists evaluate in making their investment decisions, the aforementioned categories were reduced into three primary factors: (1) management qualifications (people), (2) financial projections and related market information (financials), (3) potential exit opportunities (exit). The selection of these three primary factors was based in part on the statements made by the venture capitalists during the interview process in which they explained their response to proposals in terms of gut reaction, liking the product, and liking the management team.

The three hypothetical venture proposals for this study were written so as to appear competitive with actual proposals which cross a venture capitalist's desk daily. All the product ideas were based in reality in that some prototype existed either in technical literature or in another marketplace; however, none of the companies actually existed in any form. All three proposals contained the eight categories of information mentioned earlier as being demanded by most financiers. The first proposal, Consumer Lasers, Inc. (CLI), represents an existing industrial technology which is to be introduced to the consumer market for the first time. The second proposal, Suntan, Inc. (SI), represents an existing technological product which is to be reintroduced to the consumer market through a unique marketing approach. The third proposal, Tissue Reproduction, Inc. (TRI), represents a new technology which has just been developed and is now ready to be put into the professional (service) marketplace. All three proposals differ from each other in design. They share the same eight information categories; however, the specific information is unique to each proposal.

The three primary factors mentioned above—people, financials, exit—were used to assist in creating the categories for the venture capitalists' comments. In order to elicit information, each of the three factors was varied at two levels—"present" and "absent." Not all of the factor information was eliminated when it was considered to be absent; however, enough of the information was removed to make the proposal seem more risky. It was felt that had all of the particular factor information been eliminated, the proposal would not have been taken seriously.

Each venture capitalist participating in the study was to receive a copy of each of the three venture proposals. Each proposal was written in seven different versions, determined by the presence/absence of the three factors:

Figure 3. Proposal Versions

Version Number	People	Factor Financials	Exit
1	+	+	+
2	+	-	-
3	+	+	-
4	+	-	+
5	-	+	+
6	-	+	-
7	-	-	+

where + = present
- = absent

Only seven versions were written since it was felt that if all three factors were absent in any one proposal, the venture capitalist would reject the proposal immediately.

In order to take advantage of any information which might be gained through the use of the primary factors, a 3×3 Graeco-Latin square design with one replication was chosen. The basic design can be illustrated as follows:

Figure 4. Research Design Illustration

Venture Capitalist Number	Factor	Level of Factors In the Proposal CLI	SI	TRI
1	People	A	B	C
2	Financials	B	C	A
3	Exit	C	A	B

where A = only one factor present (the one indicated)
B = two factors present (the one indicated is absent)
C = all three factors present

The case of all three factors at the same level in all three proposals being given to any one venture capitalist was eliminated since virtually the same information could be retrieved through data analysis.

The 3×3 Graeco-Latin square in general is as follows:

$A\alpha$	$B\beta$	$C\gamma$
$B\gamma$	$C\alpha$	$A\beta$
$C\beta$	$A\gamma$	$B\alpha$

In this study, the factors followed the Graeco square and the proposals followed the Latin square. All permutations of rows and columns yield twelve different 3×3 Latin squares; however, these twelve have the same partitioning in sets of three. For this reason, only two distinct partitions of the nine cells actually exist. The design, then, can be shown as follows:

Figure 5. Partitions of the Research Design

Partition 1:				Partition 2:			
Venture Capitalist ID Number	**Proposals 1**	**2**	**3**	**Venture Capitalist ID Number**	**Proposals 1**	**2**	**3**
1.	$A\alpha$	$B\alpha$	$C\alpha$	10.	$A\alpha$	$B\alpha$	$C\alpha$
2.	$B\beta$	$C\beta$	$A\beta$	11.	$C\beta$	$A\beta$	$B\beta$
3.	$C\gamma$	$A\gamma$	$B\gamma$	12.	$B\gamma$	$C\gamma$	$A\gamma$
4.	$A\gamma$	$B\gamma$	$C\gamma$	13.	$A\gamma$	$B\gamma$	$C\gamma$
5.	$B\alpha$	$C\alpha$	$A\alpha$	14.	$C\alpha$	$A\alpha$	$B\alpha$
6.	$C\beta$	$A\beta$	$B\beta$	15.	$B\beta$	$C\beta$	$A\beta$
7.	$A\beta$	$B\beta$	$C\beta$	16.	$A\beta$	$B\beta$	$C\beta$
8.	$B\gamma$	$C\gamma$	$A\gamma$	17.	$C\gamma$	$A\gamma$	$B\gamma$
9.	$C\alpha$	$A\alpha$	$B\alpha$	18.	$B\alpha$	$C\alpha$	$A\alpha$

where A = one factor present (the one indicated)
B = two factors present (not the one indicated)
C = all three factors present
α = exit
β = people
γ = financials

This design, then, requires eighteen venture capitalist participants for each replication. With one replication, the total number of participants needed is thirty-six.

Notice that C with any of the Graeco factors (α, β, γ) has no meaning since C (all three factors present), by definition, includes all three factors. The end result is that one-third of all the proposals will have all factors present; one-third will have two factors present; and one-third will have one factor present. Specifically, the versions of the proposal now can be shown as follows:

Figure 6. Research Design Versions Grouped by Factors

Aα	=	Version 7	
Aβ	=	Version 2	One factor present (the one
Aγ	=	Version 6	indicated by the Greek letter)
Bα	=	Version 3	
Bβ	=	Version 5	Two factors present (not the one
Bγ	=	Version 4	indicated by the Greek letter)
Cα	=	Version 1	
Cβ	=	Version 1	All three factors present
Cγ	=	Version 1	

With one replication, this design yields the following number of like cells:

Figure 7. Like Cells in the Research Design

Graeco-Latin	**CLI**	**SI**	**TRI**
Aα	4	4	4
Bα	4	4	4
Cα + β + γ	12	12	12
Aβ	4	4	4
Bβ	4	4	4
Aγ	4	4	4
Bγ	4	4	4

All assignments of venture capitalists, factors, treatments, and proposals were made randomly. It was felt that the combination of randomness and balancing would provide some protection against unknown biases, at least in the design of the study.

Once the research documents were prepared, a package of three proposals (one version each of CLI, SI, and TRI) was mailed to each of the participating venture capitalists. The proposals were accompanied by a cover letter which asked them "to consider the three deals (proposals) independently and in the context of your (sic) current portfolio needs, liquidity constraints, and current evaluation of the marketplace and alternative investments." They were asked to decide if they would investigate the deal further, not would they finance the proposal. This is an important distinction to note because no venture capitalist could be expected to make a financial commitment of this magnitude without having met the relevant people or having seen the product and the production environment. A copy of the letter sent to each of the participating venture capitalists appears in Appendix B.

Interviews of approximately two hours in length were conducted with all participants in their respective offices. During the interview, two general areas were discussed: (1) the nature of each venture capital organization—its demographics, attributes, and general philosophy; (2) the detailed reaction of the venture capitalist to each of the three proposals in terms of the three primary factors and their relationship to the venture capitalist's concern with risk, return on investment, and liquidity. Additionally the venture capitalists were asked to order the proposals relative to one another. During the course of the interview, they were asked to order the proposals further in terms of their attractiveness to the particular venture firm for meeting its own portfolio preferences and needs. This second ordering was different than the first in that the venture capitalist could choose to dislike all three proposals in the second ordering system. In the first system, the proposals had to be ranked relative to each other without regard to their appropriateness for meeting the venture capitalist's real portfolio preferences and needs.

In general, it was intended that comments be structured around a probability assessment format in which questions were to be answered on both the probability and value scales jointly. Where no ordinal scale made sense, responses using descriptors such as high, medium, and low were requested. By structuring the responses, the encoding process (reducing qualitative statements to quantitative scales) was made easier.

Regarding the structure of the interviews, the researcher had a prepared list of general areas to be explored through the interview process: (1) personnel, (2) product, (3) exit opportunity, (4) capitalization, (5) timing, (6) gross margins. All of these areas involved issues of risk, return on investment, and liquidity. In each proposal, the nature of each area had been structured so as to be different from the other proposals. It was hoped that through the discussion, these built-in differences would help reveal the financier's biases.

Underlying the selection of these six general areas was a simulation model of the decision-making analysis much like the nine-input-variable model designed by Hertz in 1964.[3] Hertz's model divided the nine variables into three areas of similarity: (1) market analyses-market size and rate of growth, selling prices, firm's market share; (2) investment-cost analyses-service life, operating cost characteristics, other technological factors; (3) operating and fixed cost analyses-information about the firm's production function. He recognized the lack of independence between many of the variables.

Another useful structural model was presented by Scherer in his book, *Industrial Market Structure and Economic Performances.*[4] Scherer labeled it "A Model of Industrial Organization Analysis." With this model, Scherer sought to "identify sets of attributes or variables which influence economic performance and to build theories detailing the nature of the links between those attributes and end performance."[5] Briefly, the model illustrates the relationship between market performance, seller/buyer conduct in the marketplace, relevant market structure, and basic supply/demand conditions.

After the interviews were conducted, the following 21 categories were devised for recording venture capitalists' responses, using these two models as guidelines:

1. *Value to the world*—usefulness of the product, its ability to meet a real need as opposed to a perceived need.
2. *Demand growth*—degree to which the product is demanded in the marketplace, its rate of demand growth.
3. *Availability of substitutes*—degree to which substitutable products exist, degree to which these substitutes are in demand.
4. *Price elasticity*—the degree of demand change at varying product prices.
5. *Technological characteristics*—product durability, sophistication of technological components, product's physical characteristics, production process, substitutability of production process and/or parts.
6. *Marketing and advertising strategies*—plans and commitments for getting the product to the marketplace, includes dollar commitments.
7. *Product liability*—degree of potential hazardousness to the user, cost of appropriate insurance.
8. *Government regulations*—degree to which the business and its products are subject to government inspection and regulation, time and dollars associated with compliance.
9. *Research and Development commitments*—amount of dollars as percent of gross profit allocated to R and D, relationship of the R and D function to the overall business plan.
10. *Market size*—size of the market in terms of number of participants and total dollar volume.
11. *Distribution system*—method by which products leave the production system and are delivered to the marketplace.
12. *Margins*—appropriateness and adequacy of gross and net margins.
13. *Years to maturity*—appropriateness and acceptability of expected number of years for the firm to reach maturity.
14. *Capital needed*—appropriateness and suitability of the capital requirements.
15. *Percentage of market*—the actual and potential relative position in the relevant marketplace.
16. *Exit potentials*—future availability of satisfactory opportunities for obtaining liquidity, includes the time horizon for attaining such opportunities.
17. *Market barriers*—the proprietariness of the product, its ability to succeed in the marketplace, amount of marketplace competition.
18. *Profit and Loss experience*—relevant P and L experience of the chief officer(s).

19. *Technical knowledge*—relevant technical knowledge of the chief officer(s).
20. *Management commitment*—degree to which management is personally and financially committed to the new business.
21. *Management team experience*—general experience of each team member, appropriateness and relevance of the experience, overall team design in terms of experience.

For analytical purposes, these twenty-one categories were assigned either a Risk, Return, or Liquidity variable:

Figure 8. The 21 Categories: Risk, Return, Liquidity

Category	Risk	Return	Liquidity
1	X		
2	X		
3		X	
4	X		
5	X		
6	X		
7	X		
8	X		
9		X	
10		X	
11		X	
12			X
13			X
14	X		
15			X
16			X
17		X	
18	X		
19	X		
20	X		
21	X		
Total	12	5	4

The variables—risk, return, and liquidity—are not independent. Assignment of the twenty-one categories for that reason can be disputed. In making the assignments, it was assumed that although such overlapping would exist, the central issue was whether these categories helped to explain any of the differences among venture capitalists' evaluations of the three proposals—CLI, SI, TRI.

Just by the nature of the investments being considered, uncertainty pervades all three variables. In this case, Risk implies the existence of a potential cost due to uncertainty. Two types of risk generally are recognized in financial literature: business risk, and financial risk. Business risk results from the product itself and its market, whereas financial risk results from having inadequate cash funds to meet loan obligations. Financial risk affects the quality of the net income. Both types of risks are included in the variable labeled Risk.

The Return variable has two components. The first component is a measure of relative efficiency with which the firm produces its product. The second component is a turnover ratio which measures the relative efficiency of the firm's plant and equipment utilization. Ultimately, Return (on investment) should be the ratio of profits to net worth.

The Liquidity variable consists of three components. The first component, timing, involves the determination of how long the investor will have to leave his money in the enterprise. The second component, reasonable rate of return, involves the determination of a return on investment which is considered satisfactory. The third component, availability of exit opportunities, involves the determination of the potential vehicles for freeing the investor's capital for other investments. Essentially, four exit vehicles exist: (1) take the company public and sell out; (2) have the company acquired and be cashed out either by the acquiring company or through the public stock markets; (3) have the company acquire other outside financiers who cash out the current investors; (4) exercise the put-call options included in the original financing agreement papers. All of these exit opportunities assume the venture capitalist will take some form of equity position in the firm. If the financing had come as a debt package without a convertibility to equity option, the potential return on investment would be limited on the top side. Determination of reasonable rate of return would not have the same range for evaluating "reasonable," since the debt position most likely would have been taken based on a more conservative estimate of potential return. The debt position often implies a greater concern with immediate financial return on the financier's part. Most venture captialists who invest in the kinds of proposals developed for this study make equity investments, since their objective is to make as high a return on their investment as possible. They gamble on the new firm becoming wealthy, and prefer not to limit their upside potential. It is unlikely that firms such as those descibed in the proposals would be in a financial position to repay any loans early in this growth cycle. If such a financial position were the case, the firm most likely would have found less costly financing than that provided by the venture capital community.

For encoding purposes, after the entire set of interviews had been conducted, each category was evaluated by the interviewer on a five-point scale from –2 to 2. If the category was not mentioned by the interviewee during the course of the interview, it could not be evaluated, and therefore no scale value was given to that category. The –2 on the scale represented a highly negative evaluation of that category, while a +2 represented a highly positive evaluation of that category.

The score used for each of the variables (risk, return, liquidity), was calculated by summing across the categories which now contained a scaled value from –2 to 2, and dividing by the total number of categories which contained no missing values. This calculation produced an average score for each of the three variables. For each venture capitalist for each proposal, the following equations were used to determine a separate score for risk, return, and liquidity:

$$\text{RISK SCORE}=(X_1+X_2+X_4+X_5+X_6+X_7+X_8+X_{15}+X_{18}+X_{20}+X_{21})/\text{NRISK}$$

$$\text{RETURN SCORE}=(X_3+X_9+X_{10}+X_{11}+X_{17})/\text{NRETURN}$$

$$\text{LIQUIDITY SCORE}=(X_{12}+X_{13}+X_{14}+X_{16})/\text{NLIQUIDITY}$$

where X_{ij}=the score from -2 to 2 for each of the 21 categories

NRISK=the total number of risk-designated categories with a non-missing value

NRETURN=the total number of return-designated categories with a non-missing value

NLIQUIDITY=the total number of liquidity-designated categories with a non-missing value

With this scoring method, it should be noted that a positive value for a risk category meant that the category was considered low risk and conversely a negative value was considered a high risk. A positively-valued return category represented a high return potential whereas a negatively-valued return category represented a low return potential. Liquidity followed the same pattern as return in that a positively-valued liquidity category represented a high potential for liquidity; conversely, a negatively-valued category represented a low potential for liquidity. On a three-dimensional scale, then, the highest possible rating would be one where each of the three variables had a score of +2. The lowest possible rating would be where all three variables had a score of –2.

The potential for investigator bias is inherent in such a study. The bias which results from conducting the interviews—the learning/experience curve bias—could not be avoided, despite the trial run in which three venture capitalists who were not a part of the study participated. The known pool of appropriate investors was too small to permit much experimentation without reducing it to a number which would have been inadequate for the purposes of this study.

The other serious potential bias which is readily identified is that associated with the encoding process. Translating the qualitative statements into quantitative statements involved a great deal of investigator discretion, despite the attempt to encode using the probability assessment format discussed earlier. As has been mentioned by innumerable researchers, conducting a qualitative interview, no matter the technique employed, invariably involves subjective evaluation both by the interviewer and the interviewee. Four recognized areas of bias in the encoding process are: (1) displacement bias, (2) variability bias, (3) motivational biases, (4) cognitive biases. If a significantly larger amount of time could have been spent with each venture capitalist, it might have been possible to reduce the effects of these biases. However, asking the practitioner to take two hours out of a working day and offering no compensation other than psychic benefits associated with having contributed to an understanding of the venture community, seemed to be at the edge of being reasonable. Expecting thirty-six people to donate a full day to the project was beyond being reasonable. Given the trade-off between being able to interview a large section of the venture community on one hand and having to rely on existing data or a smaller sample on the other hand, the decision was made to opt for the former alternative and to accept the existence of the biases.

In the final chapter, a discussion of the available data bases illustrates how little is known about the venture capital community. In deciding what would be an appropriate pool of investors for this study, it was determined that a cross section of investors was needed. The selection was based on three criteria: (1) geographic location of the investor, (2) organizational structure/affiliation of the investor, (3) liquidity position of the investor's portfolio. While it was impossible to get verifiably accurate data on the last category, information gleaned from such publications as Rubel's *Guide to Venture Capital Sources*[6] and the *Venture Capital* magazine[7] edited by Pratt provided a guideline.

With the exception of one corporate pool and one limited partnership which was being formed by experienced venture capitalists, only investors who had been committed to early-round financings for longer than two years were selected for the study. In three cases, it was found through the interview that the selected investors no longer participated in early-round financings. Two of these venture capitalists were dropped from the sample for analytical purposes and replaced with others who did such financings. In the third case, no replacement could be found to participate within the time frame of December 1978–March 1979.

Table 1. Geographic Location

Location	Number Interviewed	Relative Frequency
Minneapolis, MN	5	.14
Chicago, IL-Cleveland, OH	4	.11
Boston, MA	7	.20
New York City	4	.11
Washington, D.C. metropolitan area	2	.06
San Francisco Bay area	11	.31
Los Angeles, CA-San Diego, CA	2	.06

Table 1 illustrates the variety of geographic locations represented by the participants. Because the San Francisco Bay Area and Route 128 in Boston have been traditional bastions of new, high-technological enterprise formation, more venture capitalists were known to be investing in such businesses there than in the other areas. For reasons of availability, therefore, more of the sample participants came from those two areas.

Primarily due to the emergence of Control Data Corporation in the high-technology area and several medical product company spin-offs from the University of Minnesota Medical School, Minneapolis has become a strong force as well.

While New York City continues to be a major financial center, due to the time commitment required for the review of the proposals and the interview itself, it was difficult to get venture capitalists there to participate in the study. Several of the major investors were closing financial negotiations at the time, and had available only a limited staff to conduct other business. Other geographic locations might have been included; however, it was felt that this selection provided a reasonable cross section of the major investors in early stage financings.

Table 2. Organizational Affiliation and Total Liquidity

Affiliation	Number Interviewed	Relative Frequency	Total Dollars Liquid (millions)*
Bank-related SBIC	7	.20	44.4
Other SBIC	10	.29	65.5
Partnership (not SBIC)	15	.43	201.0
Private Firm	3	.09	55.4
			$366.3

* Where venture capitalists reported their liquid funds to be unlimited, for the purposes of this study those funds were assumed to average $15 million. This involved seven venture capitalists in total: 1 bank-related SBIC, 1 Other SBIC, 3 Partnerships, 2 Private Firms.

Table 2 illustrates the variety of organizational affiliations represented by the investor group. Additionally, the chart summarizes the total liquidity of the investor group as was stated by them.

All the bank-related SBICs had a two-tier system for investing. The SBIC vehicle typically was used for smaller investments, where financing was provided in terms of a debt package. Most larger investments were handled through another fund which generally involved some type of equity participation. Estimates given of liquidity position may not be accurate since in most cases funds could be made available from other sources within the bank when sufficient need could be established by the venture capitalist. It should be noted that the two-tiered system permitted the non-SBIC funds to be used both for later round financings, and for other investments which would be disallowed by the SBA. Much of this money was funneled into merger/leveraged buy-out investments, where the potential return was less risky. It is difficult, therefore, to assess how much of that money really would have been available for investment in early-stage enterprises.

Some of the financiers in the Other SBIC category had this two-tier system for investing as well. In most of these firms the SBA-leveraged funds were used to generate operating income for the investment firm.

The Partnership affiliations generally were structured as limited partnerships with expiration dates ranging from 1981 to 2000. The average expiration date was 1987. The firms were operated by from one to three general partners who represented an average of seven limited partners. The limited partners primarily represented some sector of the finanical industry, ranging from insurance companies to banks.

The timing considerations can be extremely important for partnerships. If an average investment does not mature for five to seven years, and the life of the partnership is only ten years, then the relative position in the partnership's life cycle should make a difference in terms of new investments undertaken. Both the amount of liquid capital available and the time until dissolution of the partnership would be important factors. In fact, most of the partnerships interviewed had been reformed from previous partnerships with many of the original partners remaining in the new partnership. Investments which had not reached full potential, but still were promising, often were continued into the new partnership.

The private firms typically involved family holdings, a percentage of which were dedicated to long term investments in early-stage enterprises. Here again, funds which had been committed elsewhere in the portfolio could be made available for new venture investments, should a proposal warrant the investment. Liquidity estimates given to the researcher were based on the amount budgeted for venture activity and not on the amount liquid in the overall portfolio.

Table 3. Liquidity

$ Liquid (millions)	**Number Interviewed**	**Relative Frequency**
0 - 1	8	.23
1 - 5	6	.17
5 - 10	4	.11
10 - over	17	.49

* This category contains the seven venture capitalists who reported their liquid funds to be unlimited.

Table 3 illustrates the overall variety of the liquidity positions represented by the participants. The liquidity numbers contain the largest margin for error, since they are based entirely upon what the individual venture capitalist was willing to divulge. There was no apparent way to check their estimates against available public data. It is unlikely that the range of the liquidity scale is too low for most of the participants; however, the scale does provide a relative positioning of the participants.

In the next chapter, an analysis and interpretation of the information revealed by this study is discussed. While several questions were of interest, primarily this study was designed to help identify the variables which venture capitalists evaluate when making investment decisions.

4

Data Evaluation

In the first part of the interview, the venture capitalists stated what they look for in general when evaluating a prospective, early-stage investment candidate. Typically, their statements suggested that risk, return on investment, liquidity, and portfolio needs were the underlying criteria evaluated in making investment decisions. The second part of the interview was designed to determine if what they said they look at in general is in fact what they do look at when given specific proposals for consideration.[1] Two different measures of their reactions were used to determine the consistency between their overall response to a proposal and their evaluation of its underlying fundamental characteristics. Based on the assumption that these investors are rational investors, it was expected that their overall response to a proposal would be substantiated by their analysis of its fundamentals. In other words, it was felt that their reaction to a proposal should be in large part a result of their reaction to its fundamental characteristics and not simply a reaction based on whim. Reactions to the proposals were measured in terms of an evaluation score and a risk-return score.

The first measure of reaction to the proposal involved the venture capitalist's statement of his portfolio needs and preferences. Having had the proposals at least two weeks prior to the interview, the venture capitalists were asked to evaluate the three hypothetical proposals on two different scales. In the first case, they ranked the proposals relative to each other and not in terms of their portfolio needs and preferences. In the second case, they scored the proposals in terms of their portfolio preferences and needs. Table 4 and Table 5 illustrate the difference between the two scales in terms of the actual responses.

For purposes of data analysis, it was decided that the first scale (Rank Scale) did not reveal the venture capitalists' true evaluation of the three proposals. For instance, in the cases where they disliked all three, it was not possible to illustrate that feeling by simply ranking the three proposals relative to each other. For this study, then, only the second ordering scheme, the evaluation of preferences and needs, was used.

Table 4. Rank Scale

Rank Ordering*	CLI	SI	TRI	# Scores
A.	1	2	3	19
B.	1	3	2	3
C.	2	1	3	6
D.	2	3	1	1
E.	3	2	1	6
				35

where 1 = bottom rank
2 = middle rank
3 = top rank

* No other orderings were mentioned by the respondents.

Table 5. Preference Evaluation Scale

Dislike All Three Proposals	Dislike One or Two Proposals	Like all Three Proposals
9	25	1

where Dislike = score 1 or 2
Like = score 4 or 5
scale = 1 (low) to 5 (high)

The second ordering scheme, called preference evaluation rating (Evaluation), consisted of a five point scale:

1 = proposal would not be considered;
2 = proposal would be worth a couple of phone calls;
3 = proposal would be reviewed more carefully and phone calls made;
4 = proposal would be actively pursued as a strong investment candidate;
5 = proposal would be likely to receive financing.

As indicated in the interviews, proposals, once received by a venture capitalist, are read with general acceptance criteria in mind. These criteria, on the surface, include an evaluation of the management team, the product, the business concept, the financial position and future, the marketplace and plan for attaining marketplace appeal. Once the proposal is read, the next step generally is to make a few telephone calls which verify the validity of the business concept, the entrepreneur, and the marketplace. Once a reasonable degree of confidence in the validity of the business has been established, interviews are scheduled with the entrepreneur. At this point, if a proposal is pursued actively, it is evaluated carefully through intensive cross checking of given data with the reality of the marketplace. Discussions are held with current and potential customers to discern actual desirability of and necessity for the product. At various points throughout this checking process, the debt/equity structure of the financing arrangement is discussed with the entrepreneur. Once a proposal passes all the screenings, final financial negotiations are conducted.

In this study, however, when a score of "5" was given to any of the three hypothetical proposals, it was understood that the score was given prior to completing all the checking. The "5" meant that the financier was highly enthusiastic about the proposal and, barring any major unforeseen problems, would find a way to work with the entrepreneur and/or his enterprise until it was in shape to receive financing.

Table 6 displays the frequency distribution of the responses on the evaluation scale. This scale ranges from 1 to 5 and represents the venture capitalist's analysis of the proposal's potential to meet his existing portfolio needs in terms of his preferences. It would appear that CLI and SI failed to meet the needs of a majority of the investors interviewed.

Table 6. Evaluation Responses
(Scale 1 to 5)

Evaluation	**All Proposals***		**Individual Proposals** CLI (Prop.1)		SI (Prop.2)		TRI (Prop.3)	
	# Rel.	Freq.	#Rel.	Freq.	#Rel.	Freq.	#Rel.	Freq.
1	48	45.7	27	77.1	14	40.0	7	20.0
2	17	16.2	3	8.6	7	20.0	7	20.0
3	9	8.6	1	2.9	6	17.1	2	5.7
4	12	11.4	0	0.0	6	17.1	6	17.1
5	19	18.1	4	11.4	2	5.7	13	37.1
Total	105	100.0	35	100.0	35	100.0	35	100.0

* While the study was designed to include 36 venture capitalists, one interview was not conducted; therefore, only 35 participated in the study.

Partial aggregation of the evaluation responses into a single neutral category and two extreme categories (low evaluation of proposals 1 and 2 and high evaluation of proposals 4 and 5) shows more clearly the differences among the three proposals. (See Table 7.) Again, from their evaluations of the proposals, nearly all of the respondents felt CLI definitely did not meet their portfolio preferences and/or needs. SI was only marginally better. TRI, on the other hand, appeared to meet the needs of over half of the respondents.

Table 7. Evaluation Responses Aggregated

	Number of Responses by Proposal			
Evaluation	**Overall**	**CLI**	**SI**	**TRI**
Low (1 + 2)	65	30	21	14
Neutral (3)	9	1	6	2
High (4 + 5)	31	4	8	19
Totals	105	35	35	35

On the surface, this division of interest among CLI, SI, and TRI appeared to be consistent with the comments made during the interview in which twenty-two of the venture capitalists expressly stated that they did not, as a general rule, invest in consumer products, retail or wholesale businesses, or the entertainment industry.

In order to understand further this apparent difference in preferences among the three proposals, analysis of the responses which involved the proposals specifically was conducted. The result of this analysis was the creation of a second measure of their reaction to the proposals. This second measure was a three-dimensional scale which the interviewer developed from the venture capitalists' remarks. This scale consisted of the three variables: Risk, Return on Investment, and Liquidity as described in Chapter 3. Each of these variables was reduced to a mean score from the twenty-one categories which the interviewer devised after conducting the interviews.

Table 8. Correlation Matrix—All Proposals Together

	Evaluation	**Liquidity**	**Risk**	**Return**
Evaluation	1.00000	.39655	.64318	.62885
Liquidity	.39655	1.00000	.45021	.33250
Risk	.64318	.45021	1.00000	.59525
Return	.62885	.33250	.59525	1.00000

Table 9. Partial Correlation Matrix—All Proposals Together

	Partial Correlation Coefficients Controlling for the Effects of		
Variables	**Risk**	**Return**	**Liquidity**
Evaluation and Liquidity	.16	.16	--
Evaluation and Risk	--	.69	.69
Evaluation and Return	.65	--	.66

In order to simplify the data for analysis, Risk and Return were considered without Liquidity for several reasons. When looking at all three proposals together, the correlation matrix (Table 8) between Evaluation Risk, Return, and Liquidity illustrates the relationships between the variables. While it appears that Risk and Return correlate more highly with Evaluation than Liquidity does, a calculation of the partial correlation coefficients demonstrates the relationship more convincingly (Table 9). Again, it appears that Liquidity adds little to understanding the relationship between the scored evaluation preferences and the interview comments as scored by the interviewer. Therefore, it was decided that leaving Liquidity out of the analysis would not affect the conclusions drastically. Indeed, it would make it simpler to identify any relationships which might exist.

The scattergrams in Table 10 demonstrate the relationship between risk and return by the individual proposals and over all of the proposals. As mentioned earlier, the best joint score is one where both risk and return have a value of 2. At this point (2,2), risk would be the least and return the greatest. The joint risk, return scores on these scattergrams are illustrated with the relevant evaluation score. For example, whenever a "1" appears in the chart, it represents the evaluation score a venture capitalist gave that particular proposal. The coordinates, risk and return, where than "1" lies, represent the artificial scores which the interviewer interpreted from the venture capitalist's remarks regarding that proposal.

An examination of the scattergram for CLI reveals that the preponderance of risk-return scores falls in the fourth quadrant where both risk and return scores have the lowest value. All the evaluation scores in that quadrant have values of either "1" or "2" with the exception of one "3." Those who appeared to like CLI on the evaluation scale ("4" or "5") had risk-return scores in the first or second quadrant. From the scattergram, then, it would appear that most of the scores cluster on the low end of both the risk and return scales.

Considering that the vast majority of venture capitalists did not care for CLI, it is curious that four venture capitalists gave it a high evaluation. Not only did they score it highly on the evaluation scale, they also rated it highly on both the risk and return scales. They were consistent, at least, on both scales. However, that does not explain their apparent deviant response to the proposal. An investigation of the responses of the four individuals revealed that all of them indicated they would invest in consumer products. With the exception of one of these venture capitalists, the others indicated that they would not consider TRI (evaluation score of "1") and would not be inclined to consider SI (evaluation score of "1" or "2").

For some reason, then, the CLI proposal must have been exciting to this group of four. They obviously saw something they considered to be a positive factor which either the others did not see or else felt was a negative factor.

Table 10. Mean Risk and Return Scores with Evaluation Score

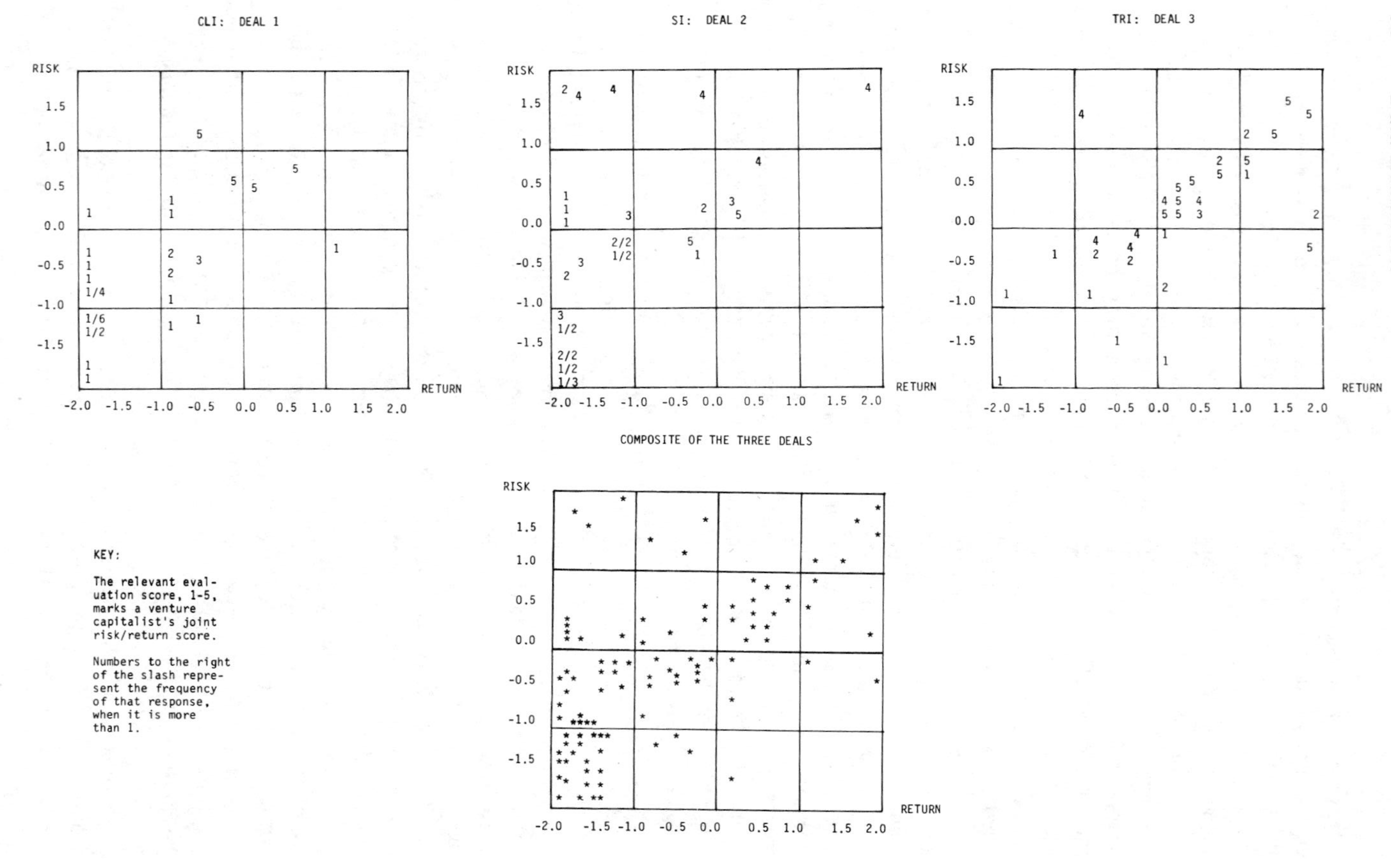

Perhaps the answer lies in a combination of liking consumer product investments and the gimmickry of this particular idea which is both technological and trendy at the same time.

The scattergram for SI illustrates much the same pattern as that for CLI. With SI, most respondents rated it poorly on the return scale; however, on the risk scale it appears to be better than CLI.

The TRI scattergram looks far different from the other two. Not only are more of the scores higher on the risk scale, they also are higher on the return scale. Out of the thirty-five venture capitalists, eighteen had risk-return scores which fell in the first quadrant. Of these eighteen, thirteen evaluated the proposal "3," "4," or "5."

Since risk and return are not independent and in fact are highly correlated with one another, it is possible to look at both the risk score and the return score by combining them into a single score. Because risk and return represent the fundamental criteria of a financial decision, it was expected that such a combined score would be a predictor of evaluation. A regression analysis was performed in order to combine risk and return. The results showed that a linear combination of .71 Risk and .52 Return was the best predictor of evaluation. These regression coefficients, then, were used to combine risk and return into a single number, an RR score, as follows:

RR Score = .71 (risk score) + .52 (return score)
where risk score = mean of risk variables
return score = mean of return variables
Multiple R = .71232.

Table 11 illustrates more clearly the relationship between the RR score and the evaluation score, where the extreme evaluations again have been collapsed into low and high. As might be expected, the line drawn at 0 RR score appears to work well for dividing the evaluations into two groups by RR score. Here again, when considering either evaluation or the artificially created RR scale, it is obvious that both CLI and SI do not meet the needs or preferences of the majority of the venture capitalists.

In order to understand better the relationship among proposal, evaluation score, and RR score, cross tabulation information was used to test several hypotheses about the relationships (see Table 12).

A histogram of the percentages in each of the evaluation cells broken down by proposal and high-low RR score suggests an interesting relationship (see Figure 9). It appears that for both CLI and SI, high evaluation score may be related to high RR score and, conversely, low evaluation score may be related to low RR score. It also appears that people may have responded differently to TRI in that more people gave it a high evaluation score but a low RR score than in the other two proposals.

Table 11. Evaluation by Risk-Return Score by Proposal

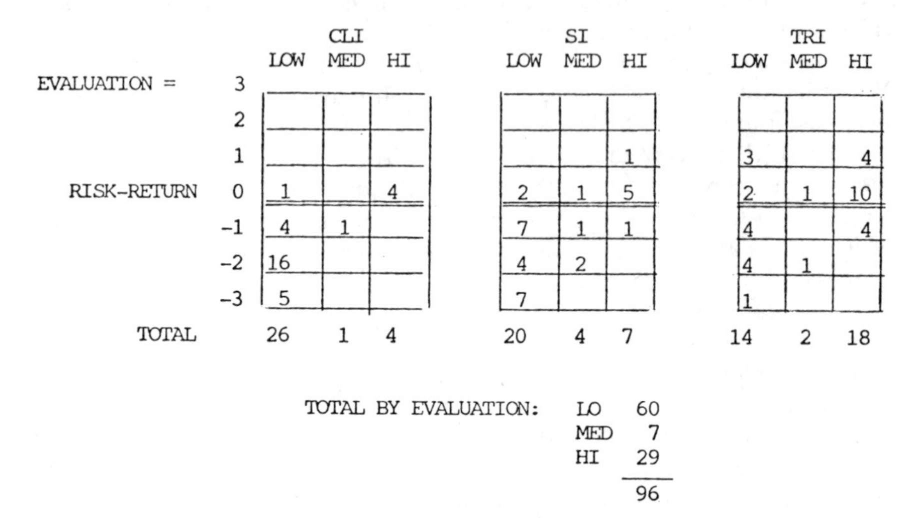

		CLI			SI			TRI		
		LOW	MED	HI	LOW	MED	HI	LOW	MED	HI
EVALUATION =	3									
	2									
	1						1	3		4
RISK-RETURN	0	1		4	2	1	5	2	1	10
	-1	4	1		7	1	1	4		4
	-2	16			4	2		4	1	
	-3	5			7			1		
TOTAL		26	1	4	20	4	7	14	2	18

TOTAL BY EVALUATION:	
LO	60
MED	7
HI	29
	96

*Because several venture capitalists had no comment about any of the return categories, their combined risk-return score could not be determined. They were left out of this analysis.

Table 12. Cross Tabulation by Evaluation Score, RR Score, Proposal

PROPOSAL:	CLI		SI		TRI			
EVALUATION SCORE:	HI	LO	HI	LO	HI	LO		
HI RR (positive):	4	1	6	2	14	5	24	8
LO RR (negative):	0	25	1	18	4	9	5	52
	4	26	7	20	18	14		89

While the small cell sizes may make the reliability of significance test results suspect, such results do suggest patterns. Because each venture capitalist responded on both the Evaluation scale and the RR scale for each proposal, it makes sense to think of the previous cross tabulation table data in terms of three 2×2 tables where the 2×2 tables consist of RR categories on one dimension and Evaluation categories on the other dimension. Each of the tables represents one of the proposals. Thus, the appropriate probability model would have nine parameters, as illustrated in Figure 10.

Figure 9. Percentage of Evaluation Scores Displayed by RR Score and Proposal

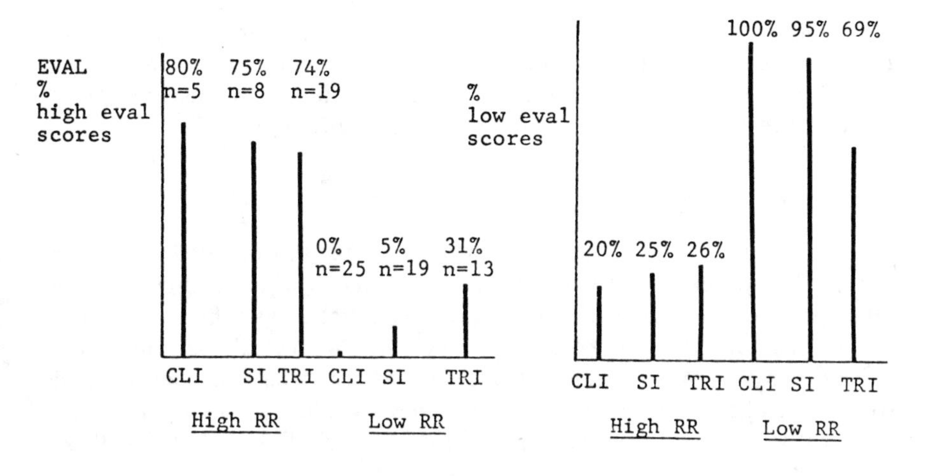

Figure 10. Probability Model

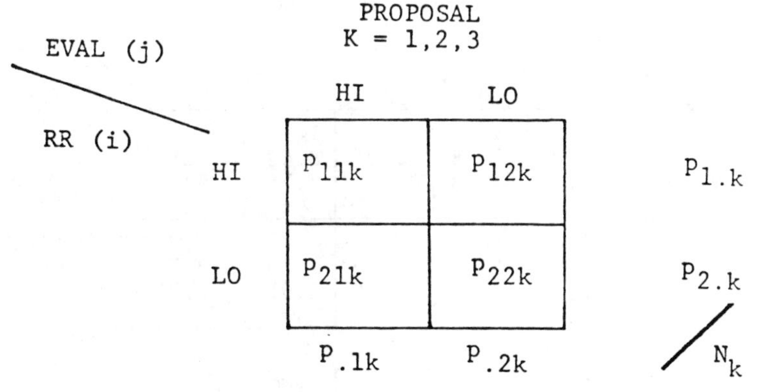

3 parameters for each k

$$H: \sum_{i=1}^{2} \sum_{j=1}^{2} p_{ijk}=1; \; k=1,2,3$$

where $p_{1.k}$ = marginal probabilities for the rows (RR score)

$p_{.jk}$ = marginal probabilities for the columns (eval score)

k = proposal (CLI, SI, TRI)

p_{ijk} = individual cell probabilities

N_k = total sample size for each proposal

Of interest is whether the responses of the venture capitalists are the same to all three proposals. Pictorially, it appears that they did react differently to each of the proposals. As a first step toward understanding the relationship among the evaluation scores, the RR scores, and the proposals, the null hypothesis can be stated that the responses of the venture capitalists to the proposals are homogeneous. In other words, the underlying distribution of responses to a proposal is the same for all three proposals.

$$H_0: p_{ij1}=p_{ij2}=p_{ij3}=p_{ij} \quad \text{for all i and j and} \quad \Sigma_{i=1}^{2} \Sigma_{j=1}^{2} p_{ij}=1$$

Since the values of the p_{ij}'s are unknown, they must be estimated. Using the pooled 2X2 results to estimate the values of the p_{ij}'s, the following table illustrates the resulting observed and expected numbers and the X^2 contribution in each cell under the above null hypothesis. The calculated value of the X^2 statistics (X^2=24.62) is quite large, even relative to what might be expected from a significance test. (X^2 for 6 df. is beyond the .005 point.) It would appear, then, that the venture capitalists do respond differently to the three proposals.

Table 13. Chi-Square Under H_0: $p_{ij1}=p_{ij2}=p_{ij3}=p_{ij}$

EVAL / RR	CLI		SI		TRI	
	HI	LO	HI	LO	HI	LO
HI	4 8.09 1.59	1 2.70 2.05	6 7.28 2.18	2 2.43 0	14 8.63 2.75	5 2.88 .92
LO	0 1.69 .83	25 17.53 2.77	1 1.52 0	18 15.78 .19	4 1.80 1.61	9 18.70 9.73

KEY:

Observed Expected X^2 contribution

The relationship between the RR scores and the EVAL scores also is of interest. One hypothesis might be that EVAL scores are independent from RR scores within each proposal simultaneously. This statement leads to the following null hypothesis:

$$H_0: H, \text{ with } p_{ijk}=p_{i.k}p_{.jk} \qquad k=1,2,3$$

Table 14. Chi-Square Under H_0: H, with $p_{ijk}=p_{i.k}p_{.jk}$

	CLI		SI		TRI	
	HI EVAL	LO EVAL	HI EVAL	LO EVAL	HI EVAL	LO EVAL
HI RR	4 .67 .12	1 4.33 1.85	6 2.07 5.67	2 5.93 1.98	14 10.69 .74	5 8.31 .95
LO RR	0 3.33 2.41	25 21.67 .37	1 4.93 2.38	18 14.07 .83	4 7.31 1.08	9 5.69 1.39

$X^2=4.75$ $X^2=10.86$ $X^2=4.16$

TOTAL $X^2=19.77$

Again, using the marginal totals to estimate the values of the parameters under H_0, Table 14 results, illustrating the observed, expected, and X^2 contribution for each cell under the null hypothesis. Each 2X2 table contributes 1 df. to the total X^2. Looking at the individual proposals first, the calculated X^2 values for both CLI and TRI are between .05 and .025 for X^2 with 1 df. SI has a calculated X^2 value which exceeds the.005 point for X^2 with 1 df. Looking at the total calculated X^2 for the three proposals, the high value relative to what might have been expected based on a significance test (X^2 with 3 df. exceeds the .005 point), again suggests that there may be some relationship between RR and EVAL scores. While this conclusion more strongly is affected by the responses to SI than to the other two proposals, there is very little reason to believe in independence within any of the proposals.

This last analysis leads to the question of the relationship between the conditional probabilities. In other words, once given one level of one score, can it be expected that response to the other score will be the same across the proposals? In order to investigate this relationship, again a null hypothesis helps to clarify the issue. The first null hypothesis is that if given HI RR, the probability of HI EVAL is the same across the proposals.

$$H_0: \frac{p_{1jk}}{p_{1.k}} \text{ independent of } k; \qquad k=1,2,3.$$

Using the pooled marginal distribution to estimate the common value, Table 15 results. Not only is the calculated X^2 value low (even on a significance test basis where X^2 for 2 df. is between .975 and .95), but in this case it would appear that when the high RR category is segregated from the low RR category, the Evaluation category substitutes well for the RR category. It seems, then, that the venture capitalists were consistent in their appraisal of the proposals on an evaluation basis given a HI RR appraisal.

Table 15. Chi-Square Under H_0: $\frac{p_{1jk}}{p_{1.k}}$ independent of k; k=1,2,3

	CLI		SI		TRI	
EVAL:	HI	LO	HI	LO	HI	LO
HI RR:	4 3.75 .02	1 1.25 .05	6 6.0 0	2 2.0 0	14 14.25 0	5 4.75 .01

X^2=.08

The other part of this picture is the conditional probability of HI EVAL given LO RR. Again, an appropriate null hypothesis is that if given LO RR, the probability of HI EVAL is the same across the proposals.

H_0: $\frac{p_{2jk}}{p_{2.k}}$ independent of k; k=1,2,3

Using the polled marginal distribution to estimate the common values, Table 16 results. In this case, the calculated X^2 value is higher than the previous case and also is higher relative to a significance test (X^2 with 2 df. is between .05 and .025). As mentioned at the beginning of this analysis, it is recognized that the presence of small cell sizes affects the reliability of significance tests.

Table 16. Chi-Square Under H_0: $\frac{p_{2jk}}{p_{2.k}}$ independent of k; k=1,2,3

	CLI		SI		TRI	
EVAL:	HI	LO	HI	LO	HI	LO
LO RR:	0 2.19 1.30	25 22.81 .13	1 1.67 .02	18 17.33 0	4 1.14 4.89	9 11.86 .47

X^2=6.81

Segregation of the RR category obviously reduces the cell sizes greatly, and therefore little credence can be placed on the strength of the significance tests. Again, they merely serve to illuminate a possible relationship which might be investigated in further research projects.

Looking at the two conditional probabilities together, it appears, then, that the results are reasonably consistent with what might have been expected in that if a proposal rated well on an RR scale, it also rated well on the EVAL scale; if a proposal rated poorly on an RR scale, it was not likely to have been rated well on the EVAL scale. The largest exception appears to be in terms of TRI where the LO RR reaction to a proposal did not deter several venture capitalists from rating it highly on the EVAL scale.

In summarizing these conditions, then, there appears to be some relationship between the RR scores and the EVAL scores for all the proposals. Theoretically, if a venture capitalist felt a proposal was appealing from the standpoint of meeting his preferences and needs (the evaluation score here), it would be expected that the investment's fundamental financial characteristics should be satisfactory as well (a high RR score here). In this study, it appeared that when venture capitalists liked a proposal's fundamental financial characteristics (high RR score), they evaluated that proposal well (high EVAL score), no matter the proposal. However, it also appeared that disliking a proposal's fundamental financial characteristics did not necessarily mean that the proposal evaluation would be low. In this case, the response to TRI appeared to be different than the response to CLI and SI.

An investigation of the responses based on the version of the proposal received for evaluation by the venture capitalist revealed little information which would be helpful in understanding this seeming contradiction. The original premise was that the different versions should make a difference in the way venture capitalists responded to a particular proposal. Basically, the seven versions can be looked at as three versions: (1) all three factors present; (2) two factors present; (3) one factor present. Table 17 displays the evaluation and RR scores by version and proposal.

Note that in general each table could have as many as twelve observations in total. Small cell sizes make significance testing meaningless, however. Table 18 displays only those cases which do not follow the rule of high RR score—high evaluation score or low RR score—low evaluation, where 0 is the breakeven point.

It appears that the version of the proposal received had little effect on the responses given by the venture capitalists. It may be that, in fact, the investor reads into the proposal what he wants to find or at least tempers his observations with his basic attraction to the proposal content. However, since there is no way of knowing at this point whether the factors varied were the ones the venture capital community considers to be the critical determinants of eventual success, it is not possible to make an accurate assessment of this possibility. Also, there is no way of knowing if those varied factors were varied enough. In other words, perhaps the situations were not made to appear sufficiently uncertain when only a few factors were present.

Table 17. Contingency Tables: Evaluation by Risk-Return Score by Proposal by Version

ALL FACTORS PRESENT		CLI		SI		TRI	
	EVAL=	LO	HI	LO	HI	LO	HI
RR SCORE	3						
	2				1	2	2
	1	1	2	1	1	1	3
	-1	1		2		2	1
	-2	5		1		1	
	-3	1		4			
		8	2	8	2	6	6

TWO FACTORS PRESENT		CLI LO	CLI HI	SI LO	SI HI	TRI LO	TRI HI
	3						
	2						1
	1		2	1	2	1	3
	-1	1		2			1
	-2	4		1		3	
	-3	3		3		1	
		8	2	7	2	5	5

ONE FACTOR PRESENT		CLI LO	CLI HI	SI LO	SI HI	TRI LO	TRI HI
	3						
	2					1	1
	1				2		4
	-1	2		3	1	2	2
	-2	7		2			
	-3	1					
		10	0	5	3	3	7

While the different versions of the proposals produced no discernable pattern of responses, this last chart of exceptions does display the original contradiction between RR scores and evaluation scores which earlier was shown statistically to be evident.

In general, two speculations can be made as to why exceptions appeared at all. In the case where evaluation was low but RR score was high, the result may suggest that a particular proposal makes sense from a fundamental perspective, but either is not the kind of investment preferred by that particular venture capitalist or does not fit his portfolio needs. In the case where evaluation was high but RR score was low, it may be that the proposal excites the venture capitalist's sense of adventure enough to warrant further consideration; however, the fundamental financial characteristics are shaky and additional information is required. In this case, the venture capitalist may be willing to try to reshape the proposal and/or company because of his enthusiasm for the people, product, or business concept. Some comments from the interviews may help to explain further the seemingly contradictory responses.

Table 18. Contingency Tables: Evaluation by Risk-Return Score by Proposal by Version—Exception Placements of Evaluations Only

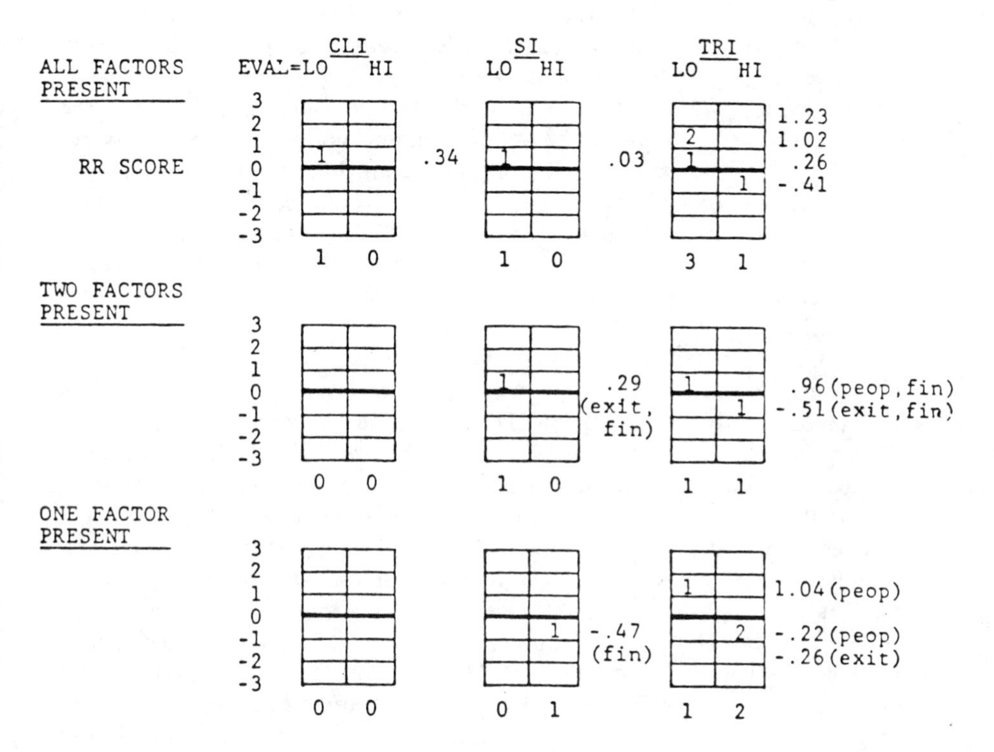

TOTAL BY EXCEPTIONS:

LO	8	(9%)
HI	5	(6%)
	13	(15%)

At the beginning of the interview, each venture capitalist discussed the kinds of investments he preferred and avoided in general. (See Appendix A for a detailed discussion of their investment preferences and strategies.) Repeatedly, consumer products, retail-wholesale businesses and the entertainment industry were mentioned as categories of investments generally avoided. The reason given for avoiding these types of businesses was that their success in a marketplace is determined in large part by the amount of advertising dollars committed to convincing the consumer to purchase the product. The products themselves generally are of a faddish nature. That is, they satisfy a preceived need rather than a real need. Most of the venture capitalists claimed not to understand the marketplace; however, it is more likely that they preferred to have their limited funds go toward filling a need which would have longevity and would not be dependent upon large marketing efforts to convince the user of its benefits or necessity.

Tied closely to the desire to finance companies whose product line is not in the consumer domain, is the venture capitalists' seeming desire to serve humanity. Medical products, for instance, contribute to the medical community's ability to save lives. To have been a part of the life-saving endeavor has much more positive social merit in the minds of the venture capitalists than having helped one more fad item reach the marketplace. Note, however, that altruistic motivations do not necessarily override the consideration of potential financial rewards.

While they often claim to prefer making investments in companies which are forging into new territories, new territory for these investors encompasses a limited domain. They repeatedly endorsed high-technology businesses. Note, however, that these businesses also have needs which are within a limited domain. Typically, start-up costs range between one-half million to two million dollars. It takes approximately five to ten years for these businesses to reach a positive net financial position; and they compete in a rapidly growing marketplace.[2] All of these factors (start-up costs, time to maturity, and growing marketplace) were mentioned repeatedly by the venture capitalists as being important characteristics of investments they preferred. Of course, it should be noted that only those venture capitalists who invest in start-up, technologically innovative companies were chosen to participate in the study. It is not surprising, therefore, that this group stated they preferred this type of investment. However, this group does represent a large portion of the known pool of venture capitalists.

Two of the three proposals given to the venture capitalists to evaluate deal with the consumer market. The home laser light show of CLI is both a consumer product and an item which may have appeal in the entertainment marketplace. SI's tan-through clothing clearly is a fad consumer item.

TRI is the only proposal which fits any of the venture capitalists' preferences for product and marketplace. Start-up costs as stated were within the desirable range; however, in reality most investors felt the costs would exceed their financial resources. Its maturity schedule as presented was appropriate; however, most felt the schedule was unrealistic. The appealing part of TRI was the product line. The potential usage for cloned cartilage is both enormous and socially beneficial. The development of such a product and the establishment of a successful company together or separately could represent major contributions to the medical industry. Not only would the product advance technology, it also would improve mankind through medical channels. The uncertainties associated with the proposal were enormous, but they were recognized by most of the venture capitalists. Curiously, the low evaluations did not necessarily match the low RR scores. Perhaps this illustrates the appeal of the product despite the uncertainties of the proposal itself.

In the case of TRI, the evaluation response to the proposal involves a desire to bring to the marketplace a product which will have enormous social impact. The venture capitalist must be willing to assume large risks in order to be a part of this process. In this study, only TRI offered the venture capitalists such a procuct and opportunity. TRI fared better than CLI and SI in terms of its overall evaluation by the venture capitalists; however, with only the one choice made available to them, it is difficult to know how it would have fared given a better selection of proposals.

From the analysis of both the qualitative and quantitative data from the interviews, it appears that some consistent relationship does exist between what the venture capitalists say about their investment preferences and the factors they actually evaluate in coming to an investment decision. It may be that many of the venture capitalists consistently rationalized their reaction to these proposals in terms of the fundamental financial characteristics. Also, the results may have been strictly a by-product of the interview process and the manner in which the data was reduced to quantitative statements. However, it is unlikely that the interviewer could have been so consistent in reducing the interviews if the patterns did not exist already. While the importance of gut reaction has not been eliminated with this study, it has been diminished. Reaction to these proposals involved a reaction to both the inherent fundamental financial characteristics and the ability of the proposal to meet portfolio preferences and needs. Further refining and testing of the methodology used in this study should lead to a more conclusive statement of the relationship between stated preferences and actual investment behavior.

5

Summary and Conclusions

The major objective of this study was to determine a set of factors which actually affect the investment decisions of venture capitalists who invest in early-stage innovative companies. Due to the dearth of information about these factors, this study proposed to begin the process of collecting such information in a more controlled manner than had been done previously. A method for data collection was created which, with refinement, might be useful in the future.

In spite of the methodological imperfections associated with studies of this kind, there would appear to be some relationship between a venture capitalist's evaluation of the fundamental financial characteristics of a prospective investment and his decision to commit resources to further investigating that proposal. While the particular definitional categories chosen to represent the fundamental financial characteristics of risk, return on investment, and liquidity may not be all-inclusive, they do help to create a measure for categorizing responses to a proposal which might hold up in future research. This study does suggest that a venture capitalist's reaction to a proposal is much more than just a gut response. While some of his reaction can be attributed to factors other than an analysis of fundamental financial characteristics, generally it appears that his investment decisions are made based on the same analysis of fundamentals as are most investment decisions. In this case, definitions of the fundamental investment criteria evaluated (risk, return on investment, liquidity) appear to be what makes the investment decision criteria seem different from those which are evaluated when more historical data exists. Had these results been otherwise, it would cast severe doubt on the usefulness of the research tool for future data collection.

While some information was revealed through this study as it was conducted, improvements in the study itself might lead to a further understanding of the investment decision process. The three hypothetical proposals were useful in eliciting conversation, opinions, and biases. Feedback from the participants indicated that, for the most part, the proposals were similar in content and format to businesss plans received by venture capitlists. While some criticism was made of the financial data and the obvious lack of a statement indicating the amount of equity offered to the investor, the basic form of the proposal was acceptable.

When designing the proposals, the major factor which had not been anticipated was the overwhelmingly negative response to consumer-oriented businesses. Because two of the three proposals involved the consumer marketplace, the sample of proposals was limited more severely in terms of potential acceptability than had been intended. Given the same or similar participant venture capitalists, in further studies the proposals should be oriented more toward the industrial marketplace. While the medical product proposal was of interest, it certainly could not be considered representative of all industrial proposals.

In designing the proposals, the factors used to create the different versions did not prove satisfactory. Either they were not the appropriate critical factors or the versions were not substantially different from each other. In other words, a stronger statement of presence or absence of each factor perhaps would have yielded different results in the interviews. Another time, it would be interesting to establish the relative significance of the written business plan to the ultimate ability of the business to receive financing. If the use of different versions of the plan were improved, more information on the importance of these plans might be obtained.

The interviews themselves were time-consuming but profitable. Having learned more about which variables are considered important, the interview time in another study could and should be reduced substantially. A more structured interview should be conducted using a combination of questionnaire and interview. The questionnaire would solicit general information about the venture capitalist and his firm, and could be included with the mailing of the proposals. The probability-assessment format did not prove to be efficient for the time available.

While the venture capitalists were not given much time to review the proposals prior to the interview, in general it was indicated that they would not have spent more time had it been available. Had they had the proposals much longer, there might have been a tendency to treat them more as case studies than as real proposals. In that event, they might have over-analyzed their comments. Since it was found that most venture capitalists meet the entrepreneurs before conducting an exhaustive analysis of the written proposal, the approach taken in this study seems appropriate for another time.

Originally, it was hoped that the results of the study would include a set of generalizable statements for entrepreneurs to use when deciding which venture capitalist to approach for consideration. Unfortunately, such a broad set of statements did not emerge. The particular sample appeared to be more homogeneous in its decision-making process than was anticipated. The demographic factors (geographic location, organizational affiliation, liquidity) used to select the participants proved not to be ones which discriminated among them in terms of their reactions to the hypothetical proposals used in this study. It is likely that by choosing venture capitalists who invest primarily in early-stage companies, the discriminatory characteristics of the demographic factors were eliminated. The one statement which can be generalized from this study is that the entrepreneur first should consider investors who are located close to the new enterprise. That is, if they want both the benefit of the financier's expertise and to improve their chances of finding adequate financing quickly, they should choose a local venture capitalist first.

It would be interesting to conduct a more intensive study, using similar techniques, in one geographic location. The San Francisco Bay area, for instance, has many venture capitalists who invest in early-stage financings, yet they do not all syndicate together on every investment. Some investments do not need the large capital commitment which generally necessitates syndication; however, others that do need syndication are not necessarily syndicated with other Bay area investors. Exploring this phenomenon might reveal more about the characteristics of the individual financier which could lead to a generalizable statement for entrepreneurs.

In conclusion, it must be reiterated that there were unknown researcher biases in designing the study, conducting the interviews, quantifying the interviews, and in interpreting the results. The effect of these biases may have been severe. Only a replication of the study by another researcher could confirm or refute this possibility. It must be noted, however, that this study was intended only as a first attempt at determining a set of decision variables. It was intended to be the first study in an anticipated series. Even assuming the existence of biases, the results appear to be reasonable.

In repeating this study, the issue of whether to conduct a clinical or a survey study must be addressed. There are benefits to both approaches; however, it should be recognized that the success of any endeavor depends upon the willingness of the investment community to participate in the study. Heretofore, little research has been conducted in the field of new business financing. It is a burgeoning area in need of academic analysis. The issues surrounding the venture capital marketplace are illusive and difficult to document. Most of the previous work done in the area has been of a qualitative nature, primarily descriptive. Most attempts to conduct useful quantitative research have been hampered by the lack of an adequate data base. No known complete set of demographics exists for the venture capital market, much less any type of longitudinal record. While each researcher attempts to create an appropriate data base, the non-existence of a common data base limits the continuity of research done in the area, whether purely theoretical or applied.

The clinical approach, then, may continue to be the more successful one for getting a handle on the major issues concerning the venture capital community. That the pool of recognized investors is fairly small suggests that it may be difficult to perform many forms of significance testing. When considering an objective approach, then, some method for increasing the number of respondents may be desirable, if not imperative. Many of the participants in this study said they chose to participate both because of the unique design of the study, and because the interviewer conducted the interviews in their offices. Many stated they were time-consuming, yet they were willing to spend two hours in an interview and several previous hours reading the proposals for this study. Most stated that they would share information for this kind of research, but were unwilling to dig through their files for the information. In other words, information would be made available only if the researcher was willing to search the files in the venture capitalist's office. Clinical studies, then, may be the more successful approach for retrieving information, given the lack of an existing data base and the difficulties associated with creating an adequate one.

Future potential research areas are numerous. Essentially, there are two directions from which to approach the field: (1) the venture capital market to the entrepreneur, (2) the entrepreneur to the venture capital market. Within each approach, there are two ways to study the issues: (1) qualitatively, and (2) quantitatively.

One area which emerges from the venture capital market to the entrepreneur approach as needing further study is the differentiation of venture capitalists in terms of their individual styles in an attempt to explain differences in investment behavior. A study of this subject might involve an investigation of the interpersonal qualities of the venture capitalist across a varied spectrum of investors. A useful source of information might be a 1972 study conducted by Hoffman[1] which began the process of identifying venture capitalist personality characteristics using a very limited cross section of the industry.

A quantitative study which attempts to measure the amount of funds available for venture investments both by investment characteristics and by financier characteristics would be useful. To date, no accurate figures exist for the number of investors in the venture capital market, much less for the amount of available capital. Additionally, no figures exist either for the types and stages of desired investments or for those actually completed. Two useful sources of information for beginning such a project might be the National Venture Capital Association (NVCA) and the National Association of Small Business Investment Companies (NASBIC) each of which has lobby representatives in Washington, D.C.

A longitudinal study of the types of proposals which do and do not receive financing would be another valuable quantitative study. Included should be the success/failure rate of both the investors and their entrepreneurial investments. This area might be approached best clinically, using well-known industry participants.

The venture capital portfolio design provides another interesting area for research. An analysis of factors which affect the overall structure of the portfolio might lead to a better understanding of the sensitivity of the portfolio to capital market conditions, economic climate, and government involvement. The federal government needs more reliable information in order to encourage the establishment of useful policy. A continuation of a study such as this one under a different set of economic indicators might be one way to approach this question of portfolio design.

In approaching the venture capital market from the entrepreneur's perspective, it first must be recognized that the problems with identification of entrepreneurial participants are overwhelming. While the entire extent of the financial community involvement in this market is not known, at least some of the major participants can be identified. On the other side of the marketplace, however, no real information source exists for locating a large sample of new entrepreneurs. This lack of information means that most studies will involve entrepreneurs who can be identified through the companies created with venture capital funds. An important fraction of the marketplace must be those entrepreneurs who were unable to obtain financing.

Given this initial identification problem, there still are some fruitful areas for research. While over the years there have been occasional clinical studies of successful, venture capitalist-financed enterprises and their entrepreneurs, a large study of those who failed might reveal some interesting investor characteristics which may have contributed to the failure. Historical records of the sixties contain many examples of such failures. Locating the entrepreneurs may be difficult, but some have begun new businesses since then and therefore still are available.

A cautionary statement must be made regarding attempts to study historical records. Few venture capitalists keep complete records. Attempts to retrieve the non-documentable aspects of investments invariably run into the problem of hazy memories. Post-game quarterbacking by both sides often ignores the realities of the past or at least tends to obscure those realities. Studies which use actual completed investments, for instance, cannot retrieve all the information and process which went into the final investment package. It is for this reason that longitudinal studies may prove to be the most useful approach for studying the venture capital market, whether from the side of the investor or the entrepreneur, either qualitatively or quantitatively.

As small business receives more visibility both in the press and in the federal government, availability of data sources likely will improve. The difficulties encountered in conducting research in the field of financing a new enterprise are outweighed heavily by the rewards of having an opportunity to do pioneering research in an area which only can serve to gain from having more visibility.

Appendix A

Investment Preferences and Strategies

In the first part of the interview, each venture capitalist was asked to list the kinds of enterprises in which he preferred to place his liquid capital. Although some had no preferences, only dislikes, Table 19 indicates a spectrum of preferences stated. It is interesting to note that as of the first quarter of 1979, the high technology and medical product enterprises were the most preferred. Cable Television (CATV) also was quite popular. These often were considered to be reasonably low risk investments with the potential to yield a satisfactory return.

While services in general, such as professional management companies, were not popular investment candidates, the services category of this study included computer software firms. Although their popularity appeared to be waning as more competition entered the field, competent technicians still were being financed.

Two other interesting observations can be made regarding investment preferences. First, it would appear from this chart that the consumer markets (retail-specialty/restaurant) were of little interest. Secondly, there appeared to be little interest in energy-related businesses. This category was considered to be separate and distinct from high-technology by the venture capitalists. This seeming lack of interest in large part was due to the instability of the marketplace for new energy. The venture capitalists felt that lack of sufficiently uniform quality standards in the new energy fields meant that the potential business risk was enormous. Most venture capitalists, therefore, were willing to let the oil companies sponsor new energy research and assimilation into the marketplace. Even though three venture capitalists specified a preference for energy-related businesses, none had made an investment in the area. At the time of the study, the federal government had made little commitment to support new-energy development, much less a financial commitment to support new-energy enterprises.

Table 19. Investment Preferences

ENTERPRISE	MENTIONED TOTAL NUMBER	PREFERENCES % TOTAL INTERVIEWED	CITY 1	2	3	4	5	6	7	AFFILIATION 1	2	3	4	LIQUIDITY 1	2	3	4	5	6
High-Technology	26	74%	2	3	5	3	1	10	2	6	6	12	2	4	5	4	11	1	1
Manufacturing	7	20%			2	1	1	2	1	1	1	5		2			4		1
Medical Products	12	34%	2		1	1		6	2	1	4	7		2	1	1	6	1	1
Cable TV (CATV)	8	23%	1		2		1	3	1	1	3	4		1	1		5	1	
Broadcasting	7	20%			3		1	2	1	2	2	3		2	1		3	1	
Restaurant	1	3%							1			1					1		
Retail-Specialty	4	11%			1		1	1	1	1	1	2		1	1		2		
Services	10	29%			3	2	2	3		1	4	5		2	2	1	3	1	1
Energy	3	9%	1			2					1	2				1	1		1
Telecommunications	4	11%	1	1		1		1			3	1		1	2	1			
Real Estate	2	6%					2				2			2					
Total # of venture capitalists possible to respond by city, affiliation, liquidity			5	4	7	4	2	11	2	7	10	15	3	8	6	4	14	1	2

CHART KEY:

City 1 = Minneapolis, MN
2 = Chicago, IL-Cleveland, OH
3 = Boston, MA
4 = New York City
5 = Washington, D.C. Metropolitan Area
6 = San Francisco Bay Area
7 = Los Angeles, CA-San Diego, CA

Affiliation 1 = Bank-related SBIC
2 = Other
3 = Partnership (not SBIC)
4 = Private Firm

Liquidity 1 = 0-1 million
2 = 1-5 million
3 = 5-10 million
4 = 10-15 million
5 = 15-20 million
6 = over 20 million

In the first part of the interview, the venture capitalists were asked how liquidity position and investment preferences are related to issues of perceived exit opportunities, potential return on investments, and timing. The standard response was that they desired a return of at least five to ten times the original investment within a five to seven year period. Most found it difficult to pinpoint the desired return; however, twenty-one were seeking an amount in excess of 25%. Seven reported actual annual average portfolio returns to be in the neighborhood of 20+%. Twenty-eight of the venture capitalists expected to make this kind of return through capital gains. Most yields from debt instruments were used merely to cover operating expenses.

In general, perceived exit opportunities fell into three areas: public marketplace, merger-acquisition, and sell-back to the management. Of the thirty-five venture capitalists interviewed, six did not feel it was important to consider exit opportunities when first evaluating a potential investment. Their argument was that if the enterprise concept was sound, an obvious exit opportunity would be available when the time was right.

Prior to the interviews, the public marketplace for new issues had been generally unenthusiastic; therefore, few felt it was realistic to count on the stock markets for potential exit. Though nearly all of the financiers would have preferred to exit through the public markets, none foresaw any change in attitude.

Nineteen venture capitalists expected that over the next several years only the merger-acquisition vehicle would be available. The intent, therefore, was to build up the new enterprise to a point where it would be enticing to a potential corporate buyer. (Interestingly, this attitude has a counterpart in the entrepreneur who feels that he will be bought out if he becomes too prosperous.)

The last exit vehicle considered by the venture capitalists, the sell-back to management, typically results from put-call options being exercised. None of the venture capitalists felt this vehicle was the best for them. It was seen as a means for exiting either a mediocre or bad investment where no alternatives were available. Seven claimed that they never would use such options in writing a contract. Such caution, they felt, meant that the enterprise was not worth the investment in the first place.

Although making generalizations about the structures of investments is dangerous since no two investment candidates are exactly alike, twenty-seven of the venture capitalists stated that they typically employed some form of senior debt/equity instrument. Those who used subordinated debentures often included an equity kicker in the financing package. Five preferred only to take equity positions with percentage ownership not to exceed 50% on their part. None of the 35 financiers wanted control of the companies through stock ownership. They all felt it was important for the entrepreneur to feel that he had control of his operation. With the exception of four, all took active board positions in portfolio companies where they were the lead investor. Active in this sense means that they act as advisers to the management team.

Several methods were employed to help mitigate against risk, in spite of the desire not to have ownership control. All 35 financiers stressed the necessity of carefully researching the potential investment. All other mechanisms served mostly as stop-gap measures for helping to survive crises.

Negative covenants covering everything from restrictions on management's ability to exit the enterprise prematurely to minimum performance criteria occasionally were written into the contracts. Again, most financiers felt such covenants served to limit management's foresight more than they served to increase the value of the financier's investment.

The single most popular method for helping to mitigate risk was the use of syndication. Except for three venture capitalists, the others felt syndication served a useful role. The foremost consideration was the relative geographic location of the potential investment. A new enterprise was a likely candidate for syndication if it was located within two hours travel time of the venture capitalist's office. An investor within the appropriate geographic perimeter would be asked to participate in the financing, and often would take the lead position.

In addition to relative geographic location of the potential investment, another important consideration in using syndication to help mitigate risk was labeled the "deep pocket" syndrome by several venture capitalists. Where a potential investment looks like it will need several rounds of extensive financing, a venture capitalist will syndicate with others in order to have a larger capital base available for these later rounds of financing. In addition to having "deep pockets" for later rounds of financing, the financier will be able to exit the investment more easily when the next rounds of money are called for if there are others in the original investor pool. Sometimes the structure of a venture capital firm may be such that there is a limit placed on the amount it can invest. If this limit is below what is necessary for the financing, others with "deeper pockets" must be brought in on the investment.

It was indicated that syndications occasionally are formed in order to acquire expertise which is missing on the firm's staff. Usually, such an individual is hired on a consulting basis, rather than being included in the investment as a financial partner.

Several venture capitalists indicated that the favor system may be another factor in deciding to syndicate an investment. Often venture capitalists have been asked to participate in investments which later turned out to be "big winners." Courtesy within the industry is to permit the same potential opportunity in return by offering an investment for syndication. How much of this favor system can be attributed to courtesy and how much to sharing the burden of risk, only the participants know for certain. It would seem logical that the largest return can be expected from the investment with the most risk; therefore, courtesy, it seems, is directly proportional to the degree of risk involved.

Appendix B

Cover Letter for the Proposals

UNIVERSITY OF CALIFORNIA, IRVINE

BERKELEY · DAVIS · IRVINE · LOS ANGELES · RIVERSIDE · SAN DIEGO · SAN FRANCISCO

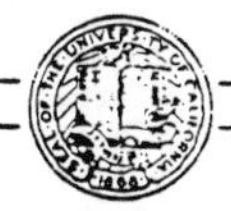

SANTA BARBARA · SANTA CRUZ

GRADUATE SCHOOL OF ADMINISTRATION

IRVINE, CALIFORNIA 92717

Enclosed are the three hypothetical venture deals we discussed on the telephone. My purpose in conducting this study is to understand what venture capitalists consider to be the most important factors in deciding whether to investigate a deal further. Please consider these three deals independently and in the context of your current portfolio needs, liquidity constraints, and current evaluation of the marketplace and alternative investments.

During the interviewing process, the nature of my questions will be determined largely by the things that impress you negatively about each of these hypothetical deals. Remembering, of course, that you cannot meet the people, please read these deals, then, to determine if each of them interests you enough to pursue it further. Assume whatever seems reasonable to you regarding things not specified.

Upon completion of the data collection, the results will be analyzed and written up for completion of my dissertation requirements. Hopefully the results will prove to be useful to both the venture capital industry and to entrepreneurs seeking funds. In no way will your comments be attributable to you personally. In order to establish the validity of the results, I ask only that your firm be identified as one of the entire group who participated in the study.

Thank you for your time and interest in my project. I look forward to meeting with you soon. In the meantime, have a happy holiday season.

Sincerely,

Christine Cope Pence

Enclosures (3)

Appendix C

The Proposals

Tissue Reproductions, Inc.

Introduction

Begun three years ago, Tissue Reproductions, Inc. now offers surgical physicians a substitute product for use in surgeries which involve replacing missing hard tissue such as bone and cartilage. TRI has developed a process whereby a small number of cells taken from the patient's body can be produced outside the body in the laboratory and grown into a tissue of suitable size for implantation in the patient where needed. The surgeon merely provides the laboratory with a small number of cartilage cells taken from behind the patient's ear. The laboratory picks up the cells, grows an inch square of cartilage from these cells, and then returns the cartilage square to the surgeon for implantation.

At this point in time, TRI grows one type of cartilage—elastic cartilage. This type of cartilage is used primarily in surgeries which involve areas of the body which will not experience excessive and continuous physical abuse. Examples of appropriate surgeries are those which involve facial repairs such as of the chin, cheek area, skull, jawbone, or nose.

TRI maintains an intensive research and devleopment program which undertakes research in the reproduction of other body tissues. Current work involves further refinement of our existing product, elastic cartilage. Within the next two years, we anticipate that TRI will offer preformed cartilage in the basic desired shapes as well as custom-made forms for such features as noses and ears. Extensive research also is being done with other types of cartilage cells, as well as with cells from bones, muscles, nerves, and special body organs.

In order to carry out our plans in a timely manner, TRI will need $600,000 in additional capital over the next two years. In addition, another $350,000 is to be placed on call should it be necessary. Dilution arrangements are to be negotiated. This proposal maps the route TRI intends to take in its business activities over the next two years under the assumption that additional financing is obtained. The following subjects are covered in this document:

— a brief history of the company
— a brief description of the current product and company operations
— a brief description of the management team
— a statement of objectives and goals
— a statement of the assumption used in designing this business plan
— financial statements and projections
— a summary of the capital needs and the intended plan for using additional capital
— an appendix containing resumes of principals.

History of TRI

Three years ago, TRI was founded by Dr. Smith and Dr. Jones. Initially, TRI operated out of Dr. Smith's medical offices with a small support staff consisting of a secretary, a laboratory technician, and a research scientist. During this three year period, the primary focus has been to obtain FDA approval for our product, cloned elastic cartilage.

In the first year, the FDA approval process was begun. Legal counsel was hired to handle the legal paperwork required by the FDA. The small research staff was hired to continue work on tissue reproduction research which is to lead eventually to our next product. The two principals, Dr. Smith and Dr. Jones, also participated in this research phase. Also during this first year, leading plastic surgeons in the nation were supplied with units of cloned elastic cartilage free of charge which they agreed to use in their surgeries. They then reported their findings in national journals and at medical conventions.

In operating out of Dr. Smith's medical offices, TRI was able to share much of Dr. Smith's laboratory equipment. To support the research, TRI obtained a foundation grant which covered the costs of the staff salaries, some laboratory equipment, and research supplies. The obligations under this grant were to supply a technical report to the foundation at the completion of the grant. The grant was provided to fund basic research in the area of tissues reproduction.

During the second year of operation, the FDA approval process continued to be the primary focus of TRI; however, during this year, an advertising campaign was begun which involved journal and direct mail media. Because the FDA process appeared to be moving ahead toward completion in the third year, it was felt that advertising at this stage would help build interest in the product sufficient to guarantee some sales as soon as the FDA process was completed the following year. In addition to the journal and mail campaigns, promotional giveaways of cloned elastic cartilage units were continued to be sent to leading surgeons across the nation. Again, it was anticipated that these surgeons would publish their findings.

Also during this second year, the foundation extended its grant from the first year. Again, the funds covered the research staff salaries and supplies. No new equipment was acquired in this year. TRI continued to use the laboratory equipment in Dr. Smith's laboratory as well as the medical facilities.

Now in its third year of operation and with the FDA approval process nearing an end, TRI is considering moving to medical facilities of its own. Dr. Bolt joined the staff mid-year as Vice President of Research. He also became a major stockholder in the corporation by contributing $75,000 in equity capital.

The advertising budget has been increased 100% to cover both displays at the major conventions in addition to journal and mail advertising campaigns. By year end, the FDA approval process will have been completed. TRI will be ready at that point to begin commercial production of elastic cartilage tissue. Due to the time frame involved in growing the tissue (two weeks), all sales orders must be made in advance and surgeries scheduled to account for this production period. Again, promotional giveaways of cartilage were continued to create further interest in the product.

The foundation grant this year continues to cover research salaries and supplies. It is anticipated that this will be the last year that this grant will be available to TRI. TRI expects to cover its research and development costs through sales in the near future.

During this first three year period, TRI has operated on funds obtained from the initial capitalization, additional equity investments in years two and three, and from the foundation grants. Initially, TRI was capitalized with $135,260 which was contributed by Dr. Smith and Dr. Jones on a 75% to 25% basis. In year two, another $80,260 was contributed on a 75% to 25% basis bringing the total capitalization to $215,520. In year three, under the same ratio, the principals again contributed a total of $130,260, bringing the total capitalization to $345,780. The third principal was brought into TRI at mid-year when he contributed $75,000 in equity. Total capitalization at year end will be $420,780.

Over the three year period, grant funds have totalled $115,000. These funds have been used in pursuing the research efforts of the company. There have been no repayment obligations to the foundation, only the obligation to produce a technical document reporting the findings of the research.

Details of the financial aspect of the company since its inception are contained in the section on financial projections.

The Product and Operations

Currently, TRI offers one product line which is the reproduction of elastic cartilage. This cartilage is taken from the patient in cellular form and then grown in the laboratory to a size sufficient for surgical implant. Technically, there are several advantages to using this form of reproduced tissues:

1. Decreased possibility for extrusion—this means that over the life time of the implant, it is highly unlikely that the implanted tissue will change form and protrude from under the skin where it was placed surgically. This reproduced tissue will remain in place without causing changes in the adjoining bone tissues.
2. Decreased possibility of infection—because it is the patient's own tissue reproduced outside the body, the possibility for infection and ultimately rejection of the implant is very small.
3. Size of implant is limitless—not being dependent upon existing tissues which could be moved (such as ribs), and used to replace missing tissue permits greater flexibility in the surgical implant process. Because supplies of existing bodily substitutes are limited, surgical implants with this form of replacement tissue also are limited. Laboratory reproduced tissue eliminates the scarcity problem.
4. Reduces need for multiple major surgical operations—the gathering of cells and laboratory-growing them into tissue eliminates the need for a major operation to remove suitable existing tissue and then another major operation to implant that tissue. With laboratory reproduced tissue, only the implant surgery becomes necessary.

The essential materials for reproducing this tissue are obtained from two major biological supply houses which have offices in Los Angeles. At the moment, we are paying $115 in supplies to produce one unit of tissue. We expect that with increased volume this figure will drop.

Capital equipment for manufacturing the cartilage involves both basic laboratory equipment and special machines for reproducing tissue. The basic lab equipment costs us approximately $15,000 and has a useful life of five years. The cell machines, on the other hand, cost us $5,000 each and have a useful life of from 3 to 5 years. Each machine can produce one unit of cartilage tissue every two weeks. Due to the unique nature of the cell machines, we do not expect to be able to receive much of a cost reduction based on quantity buying. It is likely, however, that we will be able to develop our own machines within the next few years. Currently, we get our machines from a company in Massachusetts which requires at least six months lead time from order to delivery. Though it is possible to reproduce cells without this device, the cell reproduction machine reduces the total square footage of space by 100 fold and reduces the technician time significantly.

The production process itself takes two weeks from the time of delivery of the cells to the laboratory. Setting up of the machine with fresh cells takes a technician half a day. From that point on until the two weeks are through, it takes an assistant half an hour a day to service the process. Labor costs for this part of the production process, therefore, are minimal and diminishing with increasing numbers of unit production.

The entire process from pickup of the cells to delivery of the grown tissue takes approximately two and a half weeks. Our laboratory technician arrives at the doctor's office and collects the appropriate cells from the patient. Upon return to the laboratory, the cells are placed in the cell reproduction machine and grown for two weeks. At the end of the two weeks, the delivery van returns the cartilage unit to the doctor's office in sterile form. At delivery, the doctor pays for the cartilage unit. TRI guarantees delivery of sterile cartilage tissue which is the same tissue as was grown from the patient's cartilage cells. Any problem incurred during surgery which are of a surgical nature are the doctor's responsibility.

In addition to the production of the cartilage units for sale, TRI maintains an extensive research laboratory which both monitors the quality control aspect of the production laboratory as well as conducts research on production of forms of tissue. Currently, work is being done on other forms of cartilage tissue. It is expected that joint cartilage will be ready for submittal to the FDA for approval within the next two years. Long-term research is being done on vital organ reproduction primarily involving the pancreas. Due to the importance of this research and development function to the overall success of the corporation, a sizeable proportion of the budget is devoted to this function. Capital equipment alone is costly and extensive. Initially, $50,000 must be invested in start-up capital equipment. As the projects become more specialized, additional equipment will be necessary. TRI plans to design equipment for its purposes, but the costs even in this approach will be extensive.

The Management Team

TRI feels that it is important to have a management team which represents both the medical technology with which it is associated as well as the business arena in which it functions. The company was founded by two medical doctors who are plastic surgeons by training. The President and lead principal has had prior business experience as the founder of a successful surgical supply company in southern California. Both doctors had done primary research in the tissue reproduction technology prior to starting the corporation. Both of them have continued in the basic research upon formation of the corporation. By the third year, it became obvious that an additional member was needed who represented the professional research end of the corporation. The doctor who joined the team has both an M.D. and a Ph.D. in cellular biology. Resumes of these three principals are contained in the appendix to the business proposal.

The following organizational chart illustrates the proposed structure which the corporation will take upon receipt of the additional capital financing.

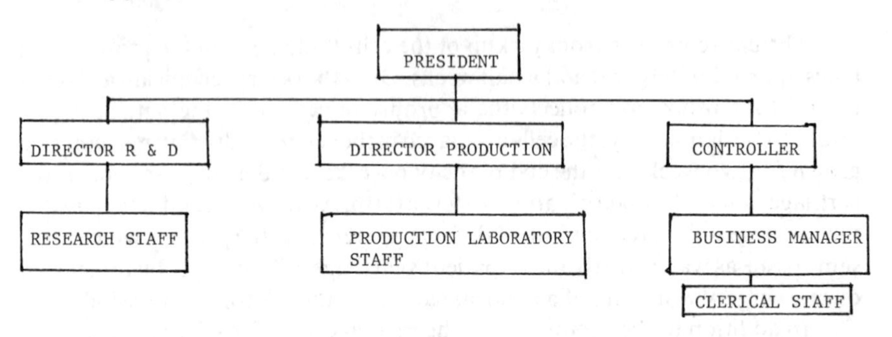

TRI believes in paying competitive salaries to its employees as a means of acquiring and keeping the best available personnel. A company profit-sharing plan is being proposed for the time when net profits are realized. At this time, employees do receive medical benefits, group life insurance, and a group pension plan as additional compensation. During the first three years of operation, the principal officers have not received any form of remuneration from the corporation except for expenses. Again, it is anticipated that they will receive a salary within the next year.

Currently, interviews are being conducted for the hiring of a business manager and the additional laboratory and clerical staff which TRI anticipates will be necessary within the year. The business manager ideally will have a masters degree in business and a proven track record. All laboratory staff will have had prior experience as well as the appropriate academic training.

For the past three years, we have had a part-time controller who has handled all our financial and accounting matters. We are negotiating with her now to take a full-time position with TRI. We intend to give her stock in the corporation in addition to a salary and other benefits. She has had previous experience as controller with a similar organization. While her responsibilities will be similar to those of a financial Vice President, we feel that she is not quite ready for that position. She does, however, have the necessary training and background to handle our needs at this point and should be a valuable asset to us in the long run as she grows with the corporation.

Objectives and Goals

Within the next few years, TRI expects to be the largest biological supply laboratory of replacement tissue in the nation. It is anticipated that over time, TRI will be in a position to acquire a large percentage of the cell and culture media distribution business as well.

In order to attain the objective of being the largest biological supply laboratory in the nation, TRI has established several operating goals:

1. *Research and Development efforts*
   This function will involve the largest capital commitment within the corporation. Primary efforts will be divided into two areas:
   1. The development of new, more efficient methods for reproducing tissues than we currently grow for the commercial market;
   2. The development of methods for reproducing all forms of body tissue which currently cannot or have not been reproduced successfully.
   The operating goal of this research and development effort is to have a new product in the FDA approval process every two years. With this goal, it will be possible to have new products entering the market place at least every two years within the next three years. Corporate profits in the early years, then, will be put into this effort rather than in large dividend payouts to stockholders.
2. *Marketing efforts*
   The basic strategy will be to advertise new products heavily in the major journals as soon as they begin the FDA approval process. It is anticipated that between $50,000 and $75,000 will be spent in the years that this process is going on. During this period, sample units of the tissue will be grown and given to leading plastic surgeons to use with the understanding that they publish an article detailing their results. As the FDA process nears completion, a massive campaign at the major medical conventions will be undertaken to promote the new product. By the time the product becomes available on the market, sufficient interest will have been developed that it can be expected to be profitable within the first year that it is on the commercial market.
3. *Educational efforts*
   TRI intends to spend time with each of its leading plastic surgeons, educating them in the use of this new product. In addition to educating these surgeons, TRI will have a regular program established whereby it conducts seminars at medical schools and large hospitals for their staff members and physicians. This educational process will lead to increased demand for future tissue replacement products.

In general, then, the operating goals will be to take all profits from sales and reinvest them in research and development efforts and in new and continued promotional efforts of existing and future product lines. Dividend payouts in these early years will be small if paid at all. In order to promote interest in this form of replacement tissue, extensive educational programs will be undertaken in addition to the advertising and promotional campaigns.

At such point that profits exceed the necessary expenses for research and development, a program for actively investigating acquisition potentials will be started. It is the intent of TRI to grow through both internal methods as well as through acquisition. Likely candidates for acquisition should be in a field directly related to tissue reproduction. These candidates include existing biological supply houses, equipment manufacturers in the field of cellular reproduction, and basic research laboratories with large grant support.

Assumptions of the Business Plan

The background assumptions of this business plan fall into three basic categories:

1. Financial
2. Market Analysis
3. Market Strategy

Financial

In developing this plan, it has been assumed that $600,000 in additional capital has been raised from an outside capital source. It is expected that this sum will be split between equity and convertible debentures with the predominant amount being in equity. It is assumed also that this $600,000 will be used wisely which will result in a financially viable corporation. By the next round of financing (approximately year six), it will be reasonable to expect the additional monies can be made available on an equity basis as needed. We would like an additional $350,000 to be on call. The financial projections shown here have assumed that the entire $600,000 was raised on an equity basis.

Market Analysis

Approximately 20,000 operations involving the elastic cartilage we reproduce are performed a year in this country. Of these 20,000 operations performed in this country, approximately 2,000 are being done in the Los Angeles and Orange County areas. A large proportion of the country's plastic and related surgeons reside in the southern California area.

Currently, alloplastic materials (synthetic plastics) such as silastic and polymers which are surrounded by natural tissue, as well as heterotopic autografts (replacement of tissue with tissue taken from another part of the individual's body) using such parts as ribs, ears, and iliac creats (hips) are the standard substances used to replace missing hard tissue. Plastics tend to either extrude after time or to waste away the bone to which they are connected. Infiltrated polymers are difficult to remove or remodel. Living tissues such as ears, hips, and ribs do not extrude; however, there is increased morbidity.

Essentially, the competition is divided between two groups of proponents:

surgeons who use alloplastic materials, and surgeons who use autografts. Of the alloplastic materials, proplast (a polymer surrounded by tissue), silastic (a solid plastic which is not surrounded by tissue), and acrylic (a medical grade acrylic) are the three primary favorites with most surgeons who use alloplastic. All of these are available through commercial companies.

Another school of surgeons prefers the autograft technique. Obviously, this has its limitations since there are a finite number of parts within the human body which are substitutable for elastic cartilage, and a percentage of these will undergo resorption (will absorb the surrounding materials and thus change form).

At this point, no other firm is producing the living tissue as we propose to do. We are unaware of any other firm even considering such an approach. We can anticipate that the biological supply houses which provide the cell cultures and media might be interested in starting such a business as ours, but to date this has not occurred. We can only surmise that they have been unwilling to do the testing and promotion which is necessary to get such a product line off the ground. Also, they may not be willing to undertake the FDA in terms of the approval process. Though this is an alternative we have chosen to take in order to protect our product and corporation from immedate direct competition, others may wish to see the outcome of the FDA approval before investing in cell production. Because of the obviously desirable features of our product such as its being the individual's own tissue, we feel that ultimately it will replace all known alternative forms of tissue replacement.

Marketing Strategy

Because no part of this tissue reproduction process is patentable, we have chosen to seek FDA approval as a means of creating lead time for ourselves in the marketplace over our competition. The entire approval process takes approximately three years. It is our intent to put all of our products through this FDA test as a technique for creating lead time. During the time that the FDA is reviewing the product, we will conduct extensive advertising and marketing campaigns to create interest in our product. Also, we will conduct an intensive physician education program at local hospitals and at the appropriate scientific meetings where new technologies generally are introduced. Leading physicians in plastic surgery will be offered free cartilage units to try. They then must continue to report on their results independent of our studies at these scientific meetings. Generally, we expect a two year turn-around from the time a doctor uses our product until the time he reports his finding to a scientific community. Because this is a slow process, we anticipate that we also will have to take on a few doctors in a formal education process, though this will become more viable later as we become recognized nationally.

Note that our intent in acquiring FDA approval is to get a jump on the competition. While we advertise during the approval period, we create demand and interest in our product. Meanwhile, competition will have to go through the same approval process if they intend to enter the marketplace, assuming, of course, that their production process is slightly different from ours. This will take them the same amount of time that it takes us, but they will not have had the advantage of being the first and most well known in the area of cell reproduction. It should also be noted, that considerable knowledge and experience has been gained by the TRI staff in the development of the reproduction process for elastic cartilage. We feel that, in fact, a primary barrier to entry into this field will be the lack of experience in this technology by others. Of course, this experience can and will be obtained so we must move quickly if we are to keep our lead.

We have considered the possibility of having detailers peddle our product much like is done in the drug industry. At this point, we feel that the cost far outweighs the potential benefits from this approach. We feel that the medical community will respond more rapidly and favorably to reports of their peers than to reports from professional salesmen.

In pricing our tissue reproductions, we have found that in order to get into the marketplace, we have to be competitive with the alternative substitutes. We therefore have priced the single units of cartilage at $600 apiece. Each piece is approximately one inch square. We feel that we can maintain this pricing schedule, assuming that we can anticipate a 60% penetration of the California plastic and related surgery market; and assuming that each surgeon does approximately ten cases a year where this type of cartilage would be an appropriate substitute. Due to the intangible benefits of this product, such as its unique nature of being the individual's own cartilage grown from his cells, we feel that there is some flexibility in price. While other substitutes may be a few dollars less, the obvious quality of our product makes it significantly more appealing. We feel that the price difference is negligible and will be covered by insurance anyway. Perhaps, costs will be lessened in the long run considering the benefits of this cartilage.

Because the laboratory's responsibility is to produce a healthy unit of living tissue and not to guarantee that the individual's operation will be successful with the use of this tissue, we feel that payment for the tissue should be made upon delivery. The number of times any one doctor will use our services in a year is limited and dependent solely upon the laws of nature and his marketing ability. We feel, therefore, that receiving payment as the cartilage is delivered should not affect the doctor's cash flow significantly, but delayed payments would affect our cash flow. Also, we do not wish to have our payment delayed should the doctor be unsuccessful in his surgery. We guarantee delivery of healthy tissue, not the associated aspects of the surgery.

All selling of the tissue will be done directly with the surgeon involved. We, the laboratory, will meet the patient in the doctor's office, where we will supervise the taking of the appropriate cells from the patient's body. We then will return the cells to our laboratory where they will be grown into the appropriate tissue size. Next, we will deliver the tissue to the surgeon's office. The entire process takes two weeks, assuming that the cells can be reproduced. Should there be a failure in the surgery, the process of retrieving the cells, growing the tissue, and delivering the reproduced tissue, would have to be repeated which would involve another two weeks. Any servicing of the tissue once it is implanted would be the responsibility of the surgeon and not of our laboratory.

At the moment, we only have one laboratory available to perform this reproduction service. While it is possible to service other parts of the country from this location, it is reasonable to expect that we will have to establish other laboratories within the near future, if we expect to remain competitive with other suppliers of the substitute products.

****

The assumptions in summary then are as follows:

1. $600,000 additional capital is acquired through a venture capital source this year; an additional $350,000 will be made available in year six.
2. The entire market consists of 20,000 operations a year nationally for the elastic cartilage units we are currently reproducing.
3. Current competition is divided between proponents of alloplastic materials for implants and of autografts which involve using the individual's own substitutable tissue.
4. The use of FDA approval process will provide us with a three year lead on the competition which will act as a patent might in the short run.
5. We are responsible only for the delivery of healthy, sterile tissue and are not liable for any aspect of the surgical procedure.
6. Our price will remain competitive on the high side since our product has obvious aesthetic value which cannot be measured in dollars. Insurance policies will cover the primary costs for the individual.

Financial Projections

Income and balance sheet statements for years one and two show actual figures. The necessary capital to get the corporation going in these years was put up on a 75% to 25% ratio by Drs. Smith and Jones in the amount of $135,260 in year one and $80,260 additional in year two. In these first two years, the product was undergoing FDA approval and therefore no sales could be made of the cartilage.

Instead, promotional units were grown and distributed to leading plastic surgeons across the country. Two units per month (24 per year) were given away. An advertising campaign was begun in the major journals in the second year. This campaign amounted to $50,000 in expenses. Over the two year period, stockholders' equity was reduced from total capital stock of $215,520 and $104,500. Foundation grants in the amounts of $45,000 and then $35,000 funded most of the research during this period.

In year three, an additional stockholder joined the corporation bringing with him an additional $75,000 in capital for the corporation. The income and balance sheet statements for year three are estimated since the year is not completed. Again, in year three, no sales can be made of the product since the FDA approval process will not be completed until year end. Again, 24 units of cartilage were given away as promotional items to leading surgeons. It is understood that these doctors will publish their results in leading journals and at scientific meetings. Advertising was stepped up this year due to the planned emergence of the product on the commercial market at the beginning of the following year (year 4). A booth was set up at the national scientific meeting to display the product and its advantages. The principals of the corporation gave lectures at that meeting on the product and talked with several leading surgeons. An extensive campaign was conducted in the leading journals to create interest. We project that by year end the stockholders' equity will have been reduced to $179,000 from the original $420,780.

Year four has been projected on a quarterly basis. We feel that this will be the most critical year in our history. Its success ultimately is dependent upon receiving enough capital in order to hit the marketplace rapidly and at full capacity. Demand will have been created already. It should be merely a matter of our ability to meet the demand. Plans for meeting that demand include renting facilities of adequate size to accomodate the full time research department as well as the production department. We are committed to renting improved warehouse space on a long term lease in Cerritos, California. The location is ideal in terms of major traffic arteries. In addition to the rent, we will be making leasehold improvements in the amount of $20,000. Primarily this will involve laboratory improvements since the front offices already are finished.

Sales already have been made for the first three months of next year (January—50 units, February—80 units, March—85 units). We have projected that the sales for the rest of the year will be as follows: April—90 units, May—95 units, June—110 units, July—110 units, August—110 units, September—85 units, October—85 units, November—60 units, December—40 units. All will be priced at $600 a unit. We expect that surgeries using our product will follow the same seasonal pattern that other plastic surgeries follow using alternative products. In order to meet these demands, we must have our laboratory fully operational immediately with basic equipment and cell machines. Because the cell machines take up to six months from order to delivery, we have ordered our supply for the year and have made the assumption that they will be made available immediately. We feel that some of these machines can be used in the research lab until such time that they are required in the production lab. Again, the projections have been made under the assumption that only two cellular units can be made by any one machine in a given month.

One of our highest costs this year will be research development expenses. We feel that this primary function will be the one that helps us stay ahead of the industry. All profits initially will be sacrificed for research and development. As can be seen by the projections, this will be a heavy expense in year four, but it will begin to even out by year five and will pay off in the long run. We intend to spend $254,000 in year four directly on research and development. We will not seek additional outside grants for this work since we feel we can cover the costs and we wish to maintain our trade secrets. Even with the additional capital requested of $600,000 bringing the total capital invested to $1,020,780, by year end of the fourth year we expect stockholders' equity to be $53,592.

Projections for year five show stockholders' equity during the middle quarters of the year, though not necessarily in large amounts. We expect that by year six, we again will have another product ready for the marketplace and through the FDA approval process. At this point, we will need expansion financing. Year end projections show stockholders' equity increasing to $308,792. Year seven projections show year end stockholders' equity of $1,455,163.

Income Statement
Years 1-3

	YEAR 1		YEAR 2		YEAR 3	
NET SALES		0		0		0
COST OF GOODS SOLD		0		0		0
GROSS PROFIT ON SALES		0		0		0
OPERATING EXPENSES:						
SELLING EXPENSES	0		0		0	
ADVERTISING	0		50,000		100,000	
OTHER	10,260		11,260		11,260	
TOTAL		10,260		61,260		111,260
G & A EXPENSES						
ADMIN. SALARIES	0		0		0	
OTHER	26,000		25,500		25,500	
TOTAL		26,000		25,500		25,500
R & D EXPENSES						
SALARIES	25,000		25,000		25,000	
OTHER	20,000		10,000		10,000	
TOTAL		45,000		35,000		35,000
TOTAL OPERATING EXPENSES		81,260		121,760		171,760
INCOME FROM OPERATIONS		(81,260)		(121,760)		(171,760)
INTEREST EXPENSE		0		0		0
OTHER OPERATING INCOME		51,000		41,000		41,000
TOTAL INCOME BEFORE TAXES		(30,260)		(80,760)		(130,760)
INCOME TAXES		0		0		0
NET INCOME		(30,260)		(80,760)		(130,760)

Balance Sheet
Years 1-3

	YEAR 1	YEAR 2	YEAR 3
CURRENT ASSETS			
CASH/EQUIVALENTS	100,000	100,450	165,900
INVENTORIES:			
RAW MATERIALS	0	0	0
WORK IN PROCESS	0	0	0
FINISHED GOODS	0	0	0
TOTAL C. ASSETS	100,000	100,450	165,900
PLANT AND EQUIPMENT	5,000	4,050	13,100
TOTAL ASSETS	105,000	104,500	179,000
CURRENT LIABILITIES			
ACCOUNTS PAYABLE	0	0	0
TOTAL C. LIABILITIES	0	0	0
NOTES PAYABLE	0	0	0
TOTAL LIABILITIES	0	0	0
STOCKHOLDERS' EQUITY			
CAPITAL STOCK	135,260	215,520	420,780
RETAINED EARNINGS	(30,260)	(80,760)	(130,760)
	105,000	104,500	179,000
TOTAL LIABILITIES AND STOCKHOLDERS' EQUITY	105,000	104,500	179,000

Income Statement
Projected Year 4

	QUARTER 1		QUARTER 2		QUARTER 3		QUARTER 4		ANNUAL
NET SALES		64,500		88,500		91,500		55,500	300,000
COST OF GOODS SOLD		80,652		117,224		125,062		115,692	438,630
GROSS PROFIT ON SALES		(16,152)		(28,724)		(33,562)		(60,192)	(138,630)
OPERATING EXPENSES:									
SELLING EXPENSES									
ADVERTISING	37,500		37,500		37,500		37,500		
OTHER	4,300		5,900		6,100		3,700		
TOTAL		41,800		43,400		43,600		41,200	170,000
G & A EXPENSES									
ADMIN. SALARIES	16,902		16,900		16,899		16,899		
OTHER	28,356		28,354		28,353		28,353		
TOTAL		45,258		45,254		45,252		45,252	181,016
R & D EXPENSES									
SALARIES	51,000		51,000		51,000		51,000		
OTHER	12,501		12,501		12,500		12,498		
TOTAL		63,501		63,501		63,500		63,498	254,000
TOTAL OPERATING EXPENSES		150,559		152,155		152,352		149,950	605,016
INCOME FROM OPERATIONS		(166,711)		(180,879)		(185,914)		(210,142)	(743,646)
INTEREST EXPENSE		(3,990)		(3,990)		(3,990)		(3,992)	(15,962)
OTHER OPERATING INCOME		9,800		9,000		8,400		7,000	34,200
TOTAL INCOME BEFORE TAXES		(160,901)		(175,869)		(181,504)		(207,134)	(725,408)
INCOME TAXES		0		0		0		0	0
NET INCOME		(160,901)		(175,869)		(181,504)		(207,134)	(725,408)

Balance Sheet
Projected Year 4

	QUARTER 1	QUARTER 2	QUARTER 3	QUARTER 4
CURRENT ASSETS				
CASH/EQUIVALENTS	628,636	450,536	273,490	75,240
INVENTORIES:				
RAW MATERIALS	10,350	12,650	9,775	9,200
WORK IN PROCESS	17,111	20,481	20,507	18,318
FINISHED GOODS	17,111	20,481	20,507	18,318
TOTAL C. ASSETS	673,208	504,148	324,279	121,076
PLANT AND EQUIPMENT	351,177	335,354	321,533	306,716
TOTAL ASSETS	1,024,385	840,502	645,812	427,792
CURRENT LIABILITIES				
ACCOUNTS PAYABLE	10,350	12,650	9,775	9,200
TOTAL C. LIABILITIES	10,350	12,650	9,775	9,200
NOTES PAYABLE	395,936	385,622	375,311	365,000
TOTAL LIABILITIES	406,286	398,272	385,086	374,200
STOCKHOLDERS' EQUITY				
CAPITAL STOCK	1,020,780	1,020,780	1,020,780	1,020,780
RETAINED EARNINGS	(160,901)	(175,869)	(181,504)	(207,134)
	618,099	442,230	260,726	53,592
TOTAL LIABILITIES AND STOCKHOLDERS' EQUITY	1,024,385	840,502	645,812	427,792

Income Statement
Projected Year 5

	QUARTER 1		QUARTER 2		QUARTER 3		QUARTER 4		ANNUAL
NET SALES		183,000		231,000		237,000		165,000	816,000
COST OF GOODS SOLD		63,042		65,342		62,467		61,892	252,743
GROSS PROFIT ON SALES		119,958		165,658		174,533		103,108	563,257
OPERATING EXPENSES:									
SELLING EXPENSES									
ADVERTISING	37,500		37,500		37,500		37,500		
OTHER	5,490		6,930		7,100		4,950		
TOTAL		42,990		44,430		44,600		42,450	174,470
G & A EXPENSES									
ADMIN. SALARIES	16,902		16,902		16,902		16,902		
OTHER	28,356		28,356		28,356		28,356		
TOTAL		45,258		45,258		45,258		45,258	181,032
R & D EXPENSES									
SALARIES									
OTHER									
TOTAL		63,501		63,501		63,501		63,501	254,004
TOTAL OPERATING EXPENSES		151,749		153,189		153,359		151,209	609,506
INCOME FROM OPÈRATIONS		(31,791)		12,469		21,174		(48,101)	(46,249)
INTEREST EXPENSE		(3,990)		(3,990)		(3,990)		(3,990)	(15,960)
OTHER OPERATING INCOME		18,000		20,000		19,000		12,000	69,000
TOTAL INCOME BEFORE TAXES		(17,781)		28,479		36,184		(40,091)	6,791
INCOME TAXES		0		(14,240)		(18,092)		0	(32,332)
NET INCOME		(17,781)		14,239		18,092		(40,091)	(25,541)

Balance Sheet
Projected Year 5

	QUARTER 1	QUARTER 2	QUARTER 3	QUARTER 4
CURRENT ASSETS				
CASH/EQUIVALENTS	(5,005)	2,364	57,586	32,625
INVENTORIES:				
RAW MATERIALS	13,800	16,100	13,225	12,650
WORK IN PROCESS	19,630	30,630	19,630	19,630
FINISHED GOODS	19,630	30,630	19,630	19,630
TOTAL C. ASSETS	48,055	79,724	110,171	84,535
PLANT AND EQUIPMENT	363,119	344,552	325,985	307,418
TOTAL ASSETS	411,174	424,276	436,056	391,953
CURRENT LIABILITIES				
ACCOUNTS PAYABLE	13,800	16,100	13,225	12,650
TOTAL C. LIABILITIES	13,800	16,100	13,225	12,650
NOTES PAYABLE	361,563	358,126	354,689	351,252
TOTAL LIABILITIES	375,363	374,226	367,914	363,902
STOCKHOLDERS' EQUITY				
CAPITAL STOCK	1,020,780	1,020,780	1,020,780	1,020,780
RETAINED EARNINGS	(17,781)	14,239	18,092	(40,091)
	35,811	50,050	68,142	28,051
TOTAL LIABILITIES AND STOCKHOLDERS' EQUITY	411,174	424,276	436,056	391,953

Income Statement
Projected Year 6

	QUARTER 1		QUARTER 2		QUARTER 3		QUARTER 4		ANNUAL
NET SALES		412,750		542,750		549,250		471,250	1,976,000
COST OF GOODS SOLD		183,585		208,749		210,325		196,444	799,103
GROSS PROFIT ON SALES		229,165		334,001		338,925		274,806	1,176,897
OPERATING EXPENSES:									
SELLING EXPENSES									
ADVERTISING	40,000		40,000		40,000		40,000		
OTHER	4,127		5,427		5,492		4,712		
TOTAL		44,127		45,427		45,492		44,712	179,758
G & A EXPENSES									
ADMIN. SALARIES	17,747		17,747		17,747		17,747		
OTHER	29,356		29,356		29,356		29,356		
TOTAL		47,103		47,103		47,103		47,103	188,412
R & D EXPENSES									
SALARIES									
OTHER									
TOTAL		63,501		63,501		63,501		63,501	254,004
TOTAL OPERATING EXPENSES		154,731		156,031		156,096		155,316	622,174
INCOME FROM OPERATIONS		74,434		177,970		182,829		119,490	554,723
INTEREST EXPENSE		(15,567)		(15,567)		(15,567)		(15,567)	(62,268)
OTHER OPERATING INCOME		18,000		20,000		19,000		12,000	69,000
TOTAL INCOME BEFORE TAXES		76,867		182,433		186,262		115,923	561,455
INCOME TAXES		(38,434)		(91,217)		(93,131)		(57,962)	(280,727)
NET INCOME		38,433		91,216		93,131		57,962	280,727

Balance Sheet
Projected Year 6

	QUARTER 1	QUARTER 2	QUARTER 3	QUARTER 4
CURRENT ASSETS				
CASH/EQUIVALENTS	(34,714)	58,034	153,549	213,732
INVENTORIES:				
RAW MATERIALS	31,050	33,350	30,475	29,900
WORK IN PROCESS	19,250	18,018	16,360	14,783
FINISHED GOODS	19,250	18,018	16,360	14,783
TOTAL C. ASSETS	34,836	127,420	216,744	273,198
PLANT AND EQUIPMENT	978,994	946,570	914,146	881,722
TOTAL ASSETS	1,013,830	1,073,990	1,130,890	1,154,920
CURRENT LIABILITIES				
ACCOUNTS PAYABLE	31,050	33,350	30,475	29,900
TOTAL C. LIABILITIES	31,050	33,350	30,475	29,900
NOTES PAYABLE	916,296	882,940	849,584	816,228
TOTAL LIABILITIES	947,346	916,290	880,059	846,128
STOCKHOLDERS' EQUITY				
CAPITAL STOCK	1,020,780	1,020,780	1,020,780	1,020,780
RETAINED EARNINGS	38,433	91,216	93,131	57,961
	66,484	157,700	250,831	308,792
TOTAL LIABILITIES AND STOCKHOLDERS' EQUITY	1,013,830	1,073,990	1,130,890	1,154 920

Income Statement
Projected Year 7

		QUARTER 1		QUARTER 2		QUARTER 3		QUARTER 4	ANNUAL
NET SALES		900,250		1,127,750		1,134,250		1,056,250	4,218,500
COST OF GOODS SOLD		274,841		331,335		332,241		318,609	1,257,026
GROSS PROFIT ON SALES		625,409		796,415		802,009		737,641	2,961,474
OPERATING EXPENSES:									
SELLING EXPENSES									
ADVERTISING	50,000		50,000		50,000		50,000		
OTHER	4,501		5,639		5,671		5,281		
TOTAL		54,501		55,639		55,671		55,281	221,092
G & A EXPENSES									
ADMIN. SALARIES	18,634		18,634		18,634		18,634		
OTHER	30,824		30,824		30,824		30,824		
TOTAL		49,458		49,458		49,458		49,458	197,832
R & D EXPENSES									
SALARIES									
OTHER									
TOTAL		66,676		66,676		66,676		66,676	266,704
TOTAL OPERATING EXPENSES		170,635		171,773		171,805		171,415	685,628
INCOME FROM OPERATIONS		454,774		624,642		630,204		566,226	2,275,846
INTEREST EXPENSE		(19,776)		(19,776)		(19,776)		(19,776)	(79,104)
OTHER OPERATING INCOME		24.000		26,000		25,000		21,000	96,000
TOTAL INCOME BEFORE TAXES		458,998		630,866		635,428		567,450	2,292,742
INCOME TAXES		(229,499)		(315,433)		(317,714)		(283,725)	(1,146,371)
NET INCOME		229,499		315,433		317,714		283,725	1,146,371

Balance Sheet
Projected Year 7

	QUARTER 1	QUARTER 2	QUARTER 3	QUARTER 4
CURRENT ASSETS				
CASH/EQUIVALENTS	336,098	649,386	964,467	1,245,895
INVENTORIES:				
RAW MATERIALS	65,550	67,850	64,975	64,400
WORK IN PROCESS	29,534	28,041	26,792	25,375
FINISHED GOODS	29,534	28,041	26,792	25,375
TOTAL C. ASSETS	460,716	773,318	1,083,026	1,361,045
PLANT AND EQUIPMENT	1,132,047	1,092,372	1,052,697	1,013,022
TOTAL ASSETS	1,592,763	2,865,690	2,135,723	2,374 067
CURRENT LIABILITIES				
ACCOUNTS PAYABLE	65,550	67,850	64,975	64,400
TOTAL C. LIABILITIES	65,550	67,850	64,975	64,400
NOTES PAYABLE	988,922	944,116	899,310	854,504
TOTAL LIABILITIES	1,054,472	1,011,066	964,285	918,904
STOCKHOLDERS' EQUITY				
CAPITAL STOCK	1,020,780	1,020,780	1,020,780	1,020,780
RETAINED EARNINGS	229,499	315,433	317,714	283,725
	538,291	853,724	1,171,438	1,455.163
TOTAL LIABILITIES AND STOCKHOLDERS' EQUITY	1,592,763	1,865,690	2,135,723	2,374,067

Summary of Capital Needs

In order to reach a viable size before competition enters the marketplace, TRI will need $600,000 in equity captial from an outside source. As a precaution, another $350,000 should be committed for a later round of financing, with the understanding that if it is not needed, the equity stock ownership will not be further diluted.

Forecasted balance sheets indicate that by year six, TRI will be in a relatively comfortable financial position. By year seven, it is anticipated that TRI will be of sufficient size to begin its acquisition search plans. The equity capital asked for in this proposal will be used to purchase capital equipment and to finance the R & D laboratory efforts. The large capital commitment to these areas is required if TRI is to maintain its lead in this particular industry through new product development in a pioneering area. With the current management team, TRI feels confident that it can achieve its ambitious goals.

The outside investor, then, can expect to make five times his original investment in seven years, assuming the market value of the company by then is ten times earnings. The large goodwill factor at this point will be for such things as a company at the forefront of its technology with a viable and ever-increasing market. Actually, TRI at this point will be ready to enter the merger/acquisition market which will provide an excellent opportunity for rapid expansion and even greater market control.

Name	Title	Birthdate
Hanes K. Smith	Chief, Plastic Surgery	July 18, 1942

Place of Birth	Nationality	Sex
Fresno, California	U.S.	M

Education

Institution and Location	Degree	Year	Scientific Field
Univ. of Calif. L.A.	B.S.	1963	Microbiology
Univ. of Calif. L.A.	M.D.	1967	Medicine
Univ. of Calif. L.A.	Intern	1968	Medicine
Univ. of Calif. L.A.	Resident	1969	Plastic Surgery
Univ. of Calif. L.A.	Fellow	1970	Plastic Surgery

Honors

Distinguished Faculty Award Research	UCLA	1973	Cellular Implants
NIH Postdoctoral Fellowship	NIH	1973	Immunology

Major Research Interest

Cloning cells (cartilage)

Research Support

NIH grant for experimental cloning of cartilage cells 1976

Awards

Columbia Univ. Ambrose Bierce Award	Cellular Research	1975
Univ. of Chicago, Chaffin Warren Award	Aesthetics of Plastic Surgery	
Presidential Award on counteracting aging		1977

Prof. of Cellular Research, UCI	1976
Chief of Surgery (Plastic Division) UCLA	1978

Publications

Dr. Smith has published extensively in medical journals. He is a certified board member in Plastic Surgery, and has worked extensively with reconstructive surgery. In 1978 he chaired the Western Society of Plastic Surgeons at Coronado and delivered the first conclusive tests results in cloned cartilage implants.

Business Experience

Dr. Smith started and continues to oversee the Southern California Surgical Supply company, Inc., which supplies local hospitals with supplies and large machinery (on a rental basis). The corporation was begun 5 years ago and now grosses $2,500,000 a year.

Name	Title	Birthdate
Davison B. Jones	Assistant Professor Cellular Implants UCLA	July 16, 1944

Place of Birth	Nationality	Sex
Guam	U.S.	M

Education

Institution and Location	Degree	Year	Scientific Field
Princeton Univ. N.J.	B.A.	1965	Microbiology
Harvard Univ. MA	M.D.	1969	Medicine
Deaconess Hosp. MA	Intern	1970	Medicine
Univ. of Calif. L.A.	Resident	1971	Immunology
Univ. of Calif. UCI	Fellow	1974	Plastic Surgery

Honors

John F. Kennedy Memorial Award		1970	Reconstruction
NIH Postdoctoral Fellowship	NIH	1975	Immunology

Major Research Interest

Cloning cartilage cells

Research Support

NIH grant for experimental cloning of cartilage cells 1976

Awards

Hortense Peapack Award	Princeton Univ.	1972	Rhinoplasty
Colonel Harlan Sanders Award	Univ. of Kentucky	1975	Rhinoplasty
Academy of Motion Pictures	Los Angeles	1976	Rhinoplasty

Dr. Jones has been retained by the Sunkist Corporation to develop the connection between prune wrinkling and cellular diminution in human cells. He is currently assistant professor at UCI in cellular implants.

Publications

Dr. Jones has had 14 papers published in medical journals world wide on the subject of rhinoplasty.

Name	Title	Birthdate
Natty R. Bolt	Chief, R & D Micro-cells, Inc.	October 10, 1942

Place of Birth	Nationality	Sex
New York	U.S.	M

Education

Institution and Location	Degree	Year	Scientific Field
Cornell	B.S.	1965	Biology
Johns Hopkins	M.D.	1969	Medicine
Johns Hopkins	Intern-Resident	1968-1970	Surgery
UCLA	Ph.D.	1974	Microcellular structures

Business Experience

Micro-Cells, Inc.	Chief, R & D	1974-present

Honors

Ph.D. Fundamental Award	UCLA	1973	Cellular implants

Major Research Interest

Cloning cells

Publications

Dr. Bolt has published 25 papers in major medical journals internationally on the subject of cellular reproduction.

Name	Title	Birthdate
Robin N. Spring		April 10, 1948

Education

Institution and Location	Degree	Year	Scientific Field
Connecticut College	B.A.	1968	French
Univ. of Chicago	MBA	1969	Finance, Accounting
Univ. of Chicago	CPA	1969	

Experience

Touche Ross	Worked for them from 1969 to 1975 in the medical area as an auditor.
Alpha Corp (A medical laboratory supply house.)	Controller 1975 to 1977

Consumer Lasers, Inc.

Introduction

Consumer Lasers Incorporated (CLI) was begun six months ago by Dr. Alexander Lite. CLI's major product lines involve home laser light shows for consumer entertainment. These laser light shows consist of a projection system which is keyed to the user's current music system and projects visual patterns on any surface where the system is placed. These visual patterns appear to have random, abstract construction which changes on a seemingly irregular but frequent basis. The overall impact is similar to that which would be achieved by watching the flames change in a wood-burning fireplace. While our laser is a neon-helium type, we have designed other point light sources into the total unit which provide additional color and variety of pattern to the projection.

At this point in time, we have introduced one product line to the public with its accompanying products. We have introduced our high-end projector first and several pattern discs which can be interchanged as the music warrants or as the interest of the viewer changes. These pattern discs are keyed at this point to general categories of music rather than to specific tunes or artists.

We have found that these projector systems appeal to a wide variety of people, but at this point are considered to be an art form. As such, our primary buyer market has been the 28-55 age group with incomes in the $25,000 to $40,000 range. This group appears to have substantial disposal income, and yet are interested in new products which have aesthetic appeal.

While we do have patents on several aspects of our product and while there is a substantial protection in terms of trade secrets, we feel that it is imperative to stay competitive with whomever might wish to enter the marketplace. We have devoted a sizeable proportion of our budget to R and D efforts in order to maintain our lead in this area. Our next product line is ready for market, but will not be introduced until the timing is correct. This product line includes a less expensive model of the projection system. We also will have available shortly, a cassette stacker for the pattern discs. Ultimately, we feel that our major product line will be a home projection system for holograms. While research needs to be done on this product, we feel that it will be within reason to expect that it will be ready for market in four years.

Because we feel that this product should be taken to market immediately and on a relatively grand scale, we will need an additional capital investment of $350,000. These funds will be used primarily to launch an extensive advertising campaign and to fund the increase in R and D expenses which will be necessary to move toward rapid growth. This proposal illuminates some of the highlights of the plan CLI intends to follow over the next three years assuming the investment of $350,000 is obtained readily. The following subjects will be covered in greater detail in this document:

— a brief history of the company
— a brief description of the current production and company operations
— a brief description of the management team
— a statement of objectives and goals
— a statement of the assumptions used in designing this business plan
— financial statements and projections
— a summary of the capital needs and the intended plan for using additional capital
— an appendix containing resumes of principals.

History of the Company

Dr. Alexander Lite first developed the home laser light show concept ten years ago. He formally entered the manufacturing business in the beginning of this year (six months ago) using first his garage for limited production and then later a small warehouse in Costa Mesa, California. During the first two quarters in which the business has been functioning out of Dr. Lite's garage, the only production staff has been Dr. Lite and his family.

The first six months have been devoted to product testing and improvement of the production process. No sales orders were contracted nor were any models made available during the first three months for preliminary marketing. During the second quarter, sixty models were produced for placement in high-visibility locations as a promotional tool. We also devoted a small amount of money to advertising, primarily in terms of meetings with potential distributors.

Also during this period, we had several meetings with representatives of the F.D.A. in order to gain approval for the use of our laser. We met all specifications and limitations placed upon us by the F.D.A. and now have a fully approved product.

In the third and fourth quarters, we have experienced some sales interest in our product. In order to meet the production schedule, we moved our operations from the garage to a small warehouse. By the fourth quarter, we have found that we needed a half-time assembler to help us meet the production schedule before the holiday season. Due to the seasonal nature of our product, we have not needed this additional assembler until the holiday quarter.

CLI was initially founded and capitalized by Dr. Lite with $250,000. He has been the sole investor to date. It should be noted that Dr. Lite put up only 45% of his net worth in order to found the company. Details are contained in the section on the management team.

The Product and Operations

CLI's first product line consists of the home laser projection unit. The second product line consists of the preprogrammed laser pattern discs which are used on the laser projection unit. This projection unit represents the first of its kind to appear on the retail market. While popular electronics magazines have contained directions for making simplified versions of our product, no manufacturing operation that we are aware of has produced the projection units for retail use.

The projection unit itself involves some precision manufacturing. Because we have perfected this process, our product offers many advantages over the home-produced models:

1. It can be used in any room of any size. The projection system can localize the pattern or it can send the pattern spiraling around the room or ceiling using an intricate mirror arrangement.
2. The system is designed so that it coordinates the pattern with the incoming music through the use of a rotating cam.
3. The combination of the laser pattern with the other point light source creates an interesting image which provides the best features of both techniques for pattern projection.
4. The interchangeable pattern discs permits for a large variety in visual effect.
5. The unique design of the projection case provides a significant deterrent for the child or curious adult who might wish to see the laser and then cause injury to the body or eye. The rigorous F.D.A. tests lead us to believe that our system is, in fact, safe for home consumption.

The basic parts for both the projection system and the pattern discs are available though several electronic supply houses. We have made a favorable contract arrangement with a major supplier for the lasers when we buy them in bulk quantities exceeding 50 per order. The housing for the system is supplied through a private contractor to meet our specifications. The housing itself is made of high-grade plastic which is molded on a wooden frame. Some wooden trim is used for visual appeal. The other major part which we contract out is the motor used to operate the rotating cam upon which the pattern disc is placed. Again, we receive a favorable discount when we buy these motors in quantities greater than 50 at a time.

As is detailed on the financial statements, the labor necessary for putting these units together requires some training. We expect that it is reasonable to anticipate that 1-2% of our gross sales will be spent on training labor. Because of the precision instruments involved, an unlimited supply of skilled labor in this area does not exist. Once skilled, production of the units can be accomplished in less than one hour.

The pattern discs on the other hand, require little in the way of material (plexiglass and a special formula cement). The major expense in producing these discs comes in the R and D which designs the appropriate patterns and in the production which must accurately recreate these fine designs. With the advent of our new machine which will be available for use in the production facility in February, the process will become less difficult and will require merely an operator for the machine. The discs then will be produced in mass quantities in a relatively short period of time. We estimate that each disc will take less than a minute to be fitted with the pattern, once the material has been cut to the appropriate specifications.

A sizeable investment must be made in precision machinery for making both the projection system and the pattern disc. The initial capital will cover some of these costs; however, additional funds will be necessary if we are to meet our target production schedules. Details are outlined under the financial section of this document.

Distribution of our system will be handled through a network of salesmen who will sell to such stores as California Stereo, Pacific Stereo, and FedCo. We do not wish to be in the retailing side of this business at this date. We feel that these items will sell in tandem with several stereo items and therefore most appropriately should be displayed there. The pattern discs are sold currently through two major rack jobbers to record stores. Because they are coordinated with certain types of music and eventually to specific records, this appears to be the most reasonable method for distribution. We have made arrangements with both the rack jobbers and with two salesmen to distribute our products to stores with whom we have made contractual arrangements. These salesmen will continue to service these accounts while making further contacts. We expect that this current method will have to be expanded as we invest more money into advertising.

The Management Team

Dr. Lite has found from previous experience with Hewlett-Packard that it is imperative to have good people if an organization is to compete successfully.

To this end, he has made arrangements with several key personnel who will join the payroll as soon as additional financing is obtained.

Dr. Lite himself has come to this company out of the engineering field. He has been a project engineer for Hewlett-Packard for the past four years. Prior to that position, he worked as a staff engineer for HP for 4 years. His primary responsibilities with HP were in the field of laser and fiber optics.

The Director of Research comes to CLI out of the laser-fiber optics industry with ten years experience with Spectro-Physicals, where he was head of the laser research group. He has had extensive experience in this field.

The Director of Finance comes to CLI from a similar company in the Bay area. He has been controller of that company for the past five years. Prior to that time, he worked for one of the major accounting firms in the area of technology audits. He has both the C.P.A. and an M.B.A.

The Director of Production has had five years of experience directly involving laser production in the industrial setting. He has both an M.B.A and a Ph.D in laser physics.

At this point, marketing is being handled under the President directly. The search is being conducted for a top marketing person who has had experience with either the electronics industry for the consumer or with the music industry in terms of electronic equipment. We are considering several applicants for this position and should have an individual selected within the next two to three weeks.

The proposed structure of the organization upon request of additional outside financing is as shown in the following figure.

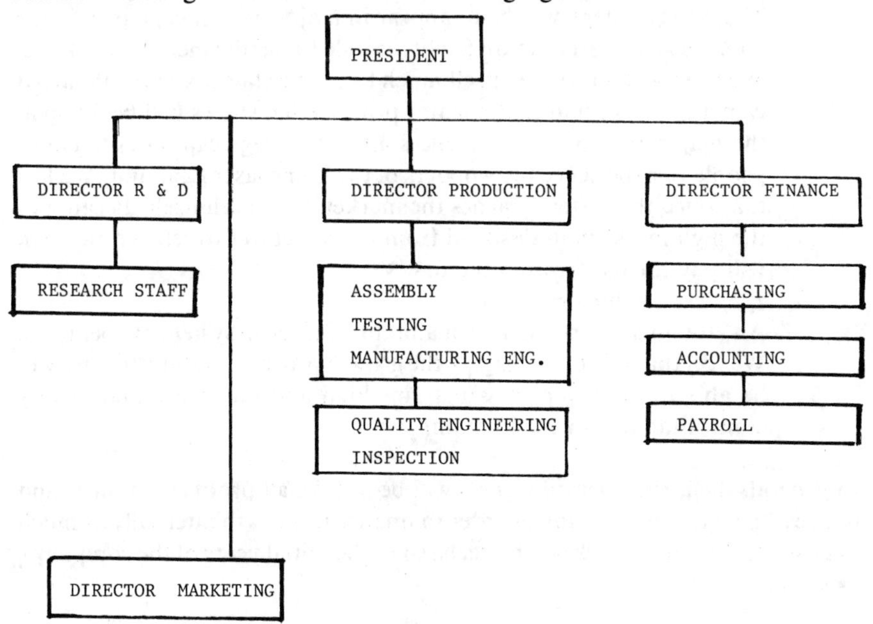

CLI believes in paying competitive salaries to its employees. Currently all employees hired are scheduled to receive medical benefits, group life insurance, and a group pension plan in addition to their salaries. Profit-sharing plans are being discussed for the day when profits are sufficient to warrant such a program.

Objectives and Goals

Within the next few years, CLI expects to be the largest and certainly the most successful of manufacturers of home laser products. It is felt that with careful planning and controlled growth, CLI can expect to maintain its competitive advantage in this area for many years.

In order to attain this objective of being the largest and most successful business of its type, CLI has established several operating goals:

1. *Research and Development efforts*
   This function will involve a substantial capital commitment relative to the overall budget of the corporation. Primary efforts will be divided between two areas: 1. maintenance and improvement of existing products; 2. development and testing of new products. It is intended that a new product or a refinement of an existing product will be introduced to the market every year with the intent being to capture the holiday market.
2. *Marketing efforts*
   The basic strategy will be to appear in major print media around the country as the production facility is able to handle increased volume. We feel the item will sell itself much like the Beta Max or the Polaroid camera. In addition to the major print media, shows will be set up at the major electronics conferences and on college campuses to entice people to experience the wonders of the home laser light unit. We feel that once the system reaches the market, it will sell itself. Because of the high mark-up in this field from manufacturer to retailer, the item will pay for itself within the first year.
3. *Efficiency controls*
   All attempts will be made to maintain an efficient system of operation. We feel that it is by managing the growth process carefully that we will be able to keep our gross margins high and our waste and quality control failures to a minimum.

In general, then, the operating goals will be to take all profits from sales and reinvest them in the company in order to finance its growth internally as much as possible. Few dividends will be declared in the initial years of the company's existence.

Research and Development efforts will be maintained to guarantee product superiority and to guarantee a steady flow of new products which will continue the process of providing products for consumer use which currently only are available in an industrial setting.

Marketing efforts will be geared toward increasing interest in the laser light show as both an aesthetically pleasing item and as an item of great pleasurability.

Assumptions of the Business Plan

The background assumptions of this business plan fall into three basic categories:

1. Financial
2. Market Analysis
3. Market

Financial

In developing this plan, it has been assumed that $350,000 in additional capital has been raised from an outside capital source. All projections have been made assuming that this entire amount has been received as equity capital, though the principal investor is open to negotiation regarding dilution arrangements. As can be seen by the financial projections, the outside investor can expect to be in a position to remove his funds by year four, should that be the arrangement we come to in the negotiations.

Also, we have made several assumptions regarding costs in developing these projections. Much of our product line involves the same kind of precision work that goes into making a mini-computer. Many of the same kind of engineers who would work in that field will be of use in this business. We, therefore used cost figures for personnel which are compatible with the mini-computer industry. We expect that our quality control and testing area also will be much like the computer industry and thus used those industry averages for our projections.

Market Analysis

While it is difficult to estimate the potential market for our laser projection system, we feel that it will be somewhat like that to which Polaroid appeals. Our major product for repeat business is the line of pattern discs which are coordinated with popular music of the day. This is similar in concept to the camera business where the major repeat business is in terms of film. We find it more than reasonable to expect sales to run upwards of 6,000 units of the projection system in all major cities over the year period. This growth will continue with the introduction of our less expensive line of projection systems.

At this point, we have no direct competition in the area of home laser light shows, however it is reasonable to expect that we will find others entering the market within the next three years. It is likely that these new entrants will compete in the low end projection system area and perhaps with pattern discs. We have patented our current style of pattern disc, however, and feel that no interchangeable disc will be readily manufactured within the near future. Our music technicians develop new pattern arrangements continually which give us a substantial bank of patterns to choose from when deciding which to market when. Also, as stated earlier, we will be introducing a unique cartridge stacking system for interchanging discs. This patented system will aid greatly in the flexibility of the machine for party use or for evening use when constantly changing patterns are desired for an extended period of time beyond the normal hour it takes to repeat in part any of the original pattern.

Reasonably substitutable products in terms of aesthetic appeal which currently are on the market are in the field of video-discs and of course television. We feel that our product is unique enough that enthusiasts of these other two media will find our product exciting as well. Our patent program, in addition to optimal engineering, should guarantee that these other two media could not be converted readily into home laser light shows. Tooling is significant enough to prohibit immediate entry into the market.

Marketing Strategy

While many of the key items in our laser show are patented, we do not feel it is safe to assume that no one else will come up with a reasonable design. Our large R and D investment is designed to keep us ahead of competition with new products. We intened to invest heavily in the first rounds of consumer interest in new products. By meeting this early interest, we will be able to charge larger prices and hopefully still realize large gross profit margins. Our R and D efforts will be geared toward developing new, innovative products using laser technology. Wherever feasible, we will seek a proprietary position with our new product lines.

Our first home laser projection system is a high end item. In order to reach the lower end of the market, we intend to introduce a less expensive model for the holiday season in year four. We believe that by that time we will have developed sufficient interest in our products to warrant offering a less expensive model. Once we bring this model to the marketplace, we feel reasonably certain that the discount houses will offer a competitive model. Since we do not feel we can compete at this level and still maintain the same profit margins, we do not intend at this time to promote heavily the less expensive lines.

Our distribution system is the key to success in this business. We have found the greatest interest in our projection system is from electronics enthusiasts who frequent music electronics stores. Because our light show adds another dimension to the audio-sensory perception which music fans find entertaining, we feel it is a natural to market our light show in tandem with stereo equipment. These stores also have facilities for darkening a small area in which our projection show can be demonstrated while listening to the music of your choice. The light show sells itself under these conditions. While we have considered marketing our product line through the major department stores much like the television games have been in the past, generally the facilities are inadequate for demonstrating the full effect of the light show. For the moment, then, we do not intend to delegate efforts in that direction.

The pattern discs are sold through independent record stores. It is our intention over the next four years to have a complete line of pattern discs for all the major music forms. We also intend to have discs available for the top ten record list. In this way, we can be reasonably guaranteed a sale of a disc with sales of top ten records—assuming of course that the consumer has our light show projection system. Currently, we are negotiating a contract with a major record producer who also has a large chain of record stores to have our discs advertised along with the promotional efforts of the studio for the release.

The pricing system at this point is based upon what the market will bear. We want to cover as much of research and tooling costs as possible in these early years. We have found that the sales outlets will markup the product price anywhere from 50% to 55% from the price we charge them. We have found that our expensive projection system can command upwards of $750 in the marketplace. Our price, then, to the sales outlet is $540. On the pattern discs, we charge $3.50; the retail outlet charges $5.50. Both items appear to be within the budget of the group to which we have appealed with our advertising (28–55 yrs. of age with incomes upward of $25,000).

Financial Projections

Income and balance sheet statements for the first year show actual data for the last quarter which is projected one month into the quarter. The original capital to get the company started was put in by the President, Dr. Lite, in the amount of $250,000. This amounts to approximately 45% of his total net worth. During the first two quarters, extensive testing was completed on the laser projection unit. Also during this period, research was being conducted on efficient methods to produce the units and the pattern discs in mass quantities in preparation for the following year when full-scale production is to begin.

During these first two quarters, CLI operated out of the garage of Dr. Lite. A small investment was made on production and test equipment. During the second quarter, sixty units were made for display in various stores as a promotional item. These units helped create the demand which was experienced in the third quarter and which currently is being experienced in the fourth quarter. By year end, we anticipate having the capital stock at a level of $312,570.

Projected statements for years two, three, and four are made with the assumption of additional capital. CLI will move into a larger production facility at the end of the first year which will permit the rapid expansion to take place that we are forecasting for the next three years. By the end of year four, total capital stock will be $1,989,917.

Income Statement
Year 1

	QUARTER 1	QUARTER 2	QUARTER 3	QUARTER 4	ANNUAL
NET SALES	0	0	55,550	167,250	222,800
COST OF GOODS SOLD	975	15,335	11,815	37,535	65,660
GROSS MARGIN	(975)	(15,335)	43,735	129,715	157,140
PROVISION FOR WARRANTY	0	0	0	0	0
MANUFACTURING VARIANCE	0	0	0	0	0
NET MARGIN	(975)	(15,335)	43,735	129,715	157,140
OPERATING COSTS:					
ADVERTISING	0	600	600	600	1,800
SALES	0	300	300	300	900
RESEARCH AND DEVELOPMENT	30,000	3,300	3,300	3,300	39,900
G & A	8,100	7,100	7,100	7,100	29,400
INTEREST (INCOME) EXP.	(10,000)	(10,000)	(10,000)	(10,000)	(40,000)
TOTAL OPERATING COSTS	28,100	1,300	1,300	1,300	32,000
BEFORE TAX PROFIT (LOSS)	(29,075)	(16,635)	42,435	128,415	125,140
PROVISION FOR TAXES	0	0	(16,218)	(46,352)	(62,570)
AFTER TAX INCOME (LOSS)	(29,075)	(16,635)	26,217	82,063	62,570

Balance Sheet
Year 1

	QUARTER 1	QUARTER 2	QUARTER 3	QUARTER 4
CURRENT ASSETS				
CASH/EQUIVALENTS	196,500	179,320	210,350	277,167
ACCOUNTS RECEIVABLE				
INVENTORIES		900	10,000	27,875
TOTAL CURRENT ASSETS		220	2,080	1,100
EQUIPMENT AND LEASEHOLD			1,020	2,100
LEASEHOLD IMPROVEMENTS	196,500	180,440	223,450	337,822
MACHINERY/EQUIP./FURN.	24,425	23,850	23,275	22,700
TOOLING	220,925	204,290	246,725	360,522
(Depreciation)				
TOTAL FIXED ASSETS				
TOTAL ASSETS				
CURRENT LIABILITIES			16,218	47,952
ACCOUNTS PAYABLE				
OTHER ACCRUED EXP.				
TOTAL CURRENT LIABIL.				
STOCKHOLDERS' EQUITY	250,000	250,000	250,000	250,000
CAPITAL STOCK	(29,075)	(16,635)	26,217	82,063
RETAINED EARNINGS	220,925	204,290	230,507	312,570
TOTAL LIABILITIES AND STOCKHOLDERS' EQUITY	220,925	204,290	246,725	360,522

Income Statement
Projected Year 2

	QUARTER 1	QUARTER 2	QUARTER 3	QUARTER 4	ANNUAL
NET SALES	122,700	296,600	360,750	587,250	1,367,300
COST OF GOODS SOLD	55,215	133,470	162,338	264,262	615,285
GROSS MARGIN	67,485	163,130	198,412	322,988	752,015
PROVISION FOR WARRANTY	2,454	5,932	7,215	11,745	27,346
MANUFACTURING VARIANCE	3,681	8,898	10,822	17,618	41,019
NET MARGIN	61,350	148,300	180,375	293,625	683,650
OPERATING COSTS					
ADVERTISING	14,724	35,592	43,290	70,470	164,076
SALES	18,405	44,490	54,113	88,088	205,096
RESEARCH AND DEVELOPMENT	12,270	29,660	36,075	58,725	136,730
G & A	17,178	41,524	50,505	82,215	191,422
INTEREST (INCOME) EXP.	(2,454)	(5,932)	(7,215)	(11,745)	27,346
TOTAL OPERATING COSTS	60,123	145,334	176,768	287,753	669,978
BEFORE TAX PROFIT (LOSS)	1,227	2,966	3,607	5,872	13,672
PROVISION FOR TAXES	(614)	(1,483)	(1,804)	(2,936)	(6,837)
AFTER TAX INCOME (LOSS)	613	1,483	1,803	2,936	6,835

Balance Sheet
Projected Year 2

	QUARTER 1	Quarter 2	Quarter 3	Quarter 4
CURRENT ASSETS				
CASH/EQUIVALENTS	39,149	39,333	39,558	38,676
ACCOUNTS RECEIVABLE	289,694	291,066	292,734	286,200
INVENTORIES	313,183	314,666	316,470	309,405
TOTAL CURRENT ASSETS	642,026	645,065	648,762	634,281
EQUIPMENT AND LEASEHOLD				
LEASEHOLD IMPROVEMENTS	39,147	39,334	39,558	38,675
MACHINERY/EQUIP./FURN.	101,785	102,266	102,853	100,557
TOOLING	15,659	15,733	15,823	15,470
(Depreciation)	(15,659)	(15,733)	(15,823)	(15,470)
TOTAL FIXED ASSETS	140,932	141,600	142,411	139,232
TOTAL ASSETS	782,958	786,665	791,174	773,513
CURRENT LIABILITIES				
ACCOUNTS PAYABLE	234,887	236,000	142,411	232,054
OTHER ACCRUED EXP.	234,888	235,999	142,412	232,054
TOTAL CURRENT LIABIL.	469,775	471,999	474,703	464,108
STOCKHOLDERS' EQUITY				
CAPITAL STOCK	600,000	600,000	600,000	600,000
RETAINED EARNINGS	613	1,483	1,803	2,936
	313,183	314,666	316,469	319,405
TOTAL LIABILITIES AND STOCKHOLDERS' EQUITY	782,958	786,665	791,174	773,513

Income Statement
Projected Year 3

	QUARTER 1	QUARTER 2	QUARTER 3	QUARTER 4	ANNUAL
NET SALES	1,277,000	1,824,000	2,212,500	2,759,500	8,073,000
COST OF GOODS SOLD	536,340	766,080	929,250	1,158,990	3,390,660
GROSS MARGIN	740,660	1,057,920	1,283,250	1,600,510	4,682,340
PROVISION FOR WARRANTY	25,540	36,480	44,250	55,190	161,460
MANUFACTURING VARIANCE	12,770	18,240	22,125	27,595	80,730
NET MARGIN	702,350	1,003,200	1,216,875	1,517,725	4,440,150
OPERATING COSTS:					
ADVERTISING	102,160	145,920	177,000	220,760	645,840
SALES	191,550	273,600	331,875	413,925	1,210,950
RESEARCH AND DEVELOPMENT	127,700	182,400	221,250	275,950	807,300
G & A	153,240	218,880	265,500	331,140	968,760
INTEREST (INCOME) EXP.	(25,540)	(36,480)	(44,250)	(55,190)	(161,460)
TOTAL OPERATING COSTS	549,110	784,320	951,375	1,186,585	3,471,390
BEFORE TAX PROFIT (LOSS)	153,240	218,880	265,500	331,140	968,760
PROVISION FOR TAXES	(76,620)	(109,440)	(132,750)	(165,570)	(484,380)
AFTER TAX INCOME (LOSS)	76,620	109,440	132,750	165,570	484,380

Balance Sheet
Projected Year 3

	QUARTER 1	QUARTER 2	QUARTER 3	QUARTER 4
CURRENT ASSETS				
CASH/EQUIVALENTS	49,503	631,184	79,777	100,473
ACCOUNTS RECEIVABLE	366,323	467,555	590,349	743,502
INVENTORIES	396,026	505,465	638,215	803,785
TOTAL CURRENT ASSETS	811,852	1,036,204	1,308,341	1,647,760
EQUIPMENT AND LEASEHOLD				
LEASEHOLD IMPROVEMENTS	49,503	63,183	79,777	100,473
MACHINERY/EQUIP./FURN.	128,708	164,276	207,420	261,230
TOOLING	19,803	25,273	31,911	40,189
(Depreciation)	(19,802)	(25,273)	(31,911)	(40,189)
TOTAL FIXED ASSETS	178,211	227,459	287,197	361,703
TOTAL ASSETS	990,063	1,263,663	1,595,538	2,009,463
CURRENT LIABILITIES				
ACCOUNTS PAYABLE	297,019	379,099	478,662	602,839
OTHER ACCRUED EXP.	297,019	379,099	478,661	602,839
TOTAL CURRENT LIABIL.	594,038	758,198	957,323	1,205,678
STOCKHOLDERS' EQUITY				
CAPITAL STOCK	600,000	600,000	600,000	600,000
RETAINED EARNINGS	76,620	109,440	132,750	165,570
	396,025	505,465	638,215	803,785
TOTAL LIABILITIES AND STOCKHOLDERS' EQUITY	990,063	1,263,663	1,595,538	2,009,463

Income Statement
Projected Year 4

	QUARTER 1	QUARTER 2	QUARTER 3	QUARTER 4	ANNUAL
NET SALES	2,230,000	3,327,500	4,425,000	5,522,500	15,505,000
COST OF GOODS SOLD	958,900	1,430,825	1,902,750	2,374,675	6,667,150
GROSS MARGIN	1,271,100	1,896,675	2,522,250	3,147,825	8,837,850
PROVISION FOR WARRANTY	44,600	66,550	88,500	110,450	310,100
MANUFACTURING VARIANCE	22,300	33,275	44,250	55,225	155,050
NET MARGIN	1,338,000	1,996,500	2,655,000	3,313,500	9,303,000
OPERATING COSTS:					
ADVERTISING	178,400	266,200	354,000	441,800	1,240,400
SALES	334,500	499,125	663,750	828,375	2,325,750
RESEARCH AND DEVELOPMENT	223,000	332,750	442,500	552,250	1,550,500
G & A	267,600	399,300	531,000	662,700	1,860,600
INTEREST (INCOME) EXP.	(6,690)	(9,983)	(13,275)	(16,568)	(46,516)
TOTAL OPERATING COSTS	1,010,190	1,507,358	2,004,525	2,501,693	7,023,766
BEFORE TAX PROFIT (LOSS)	341,190	509,108	677,025	844,943	2,372,266
PROVISION FOR TAXES	(170,595)	(254,554)	(338,513)	(422,472)	(1,186,134)
AFTER TAX INCOME (LOSS)	170,595	254,554	338,512	422,471	1,186,132

Balance Sheet
Projected Year 4

	QUARTER 1	QUARTER 2	QUARTER 3	QUARTER 4
CURRENT ASSETS	121,797	153,617	195,930	248,740
CASH/EQUIVALENTS	901,302	1,136,764	1,449,999	1,840,673
INVENTORIES:	974,380	1,228,934	1,567,446	1,989,917
RAW MATERIALS	1,997,479	2,519,315	3,213,264	4,079,330
WORK IN PROCESS				
FINISHED GOODS	121,797	153,616	195,931	248,740
TOTAL C. ASSETS	316,674	399,404	509,420	646,723
PLANT AND EQUIPMENT	48,719	61,446	78,372	99,496
TOTAL ASSETS	(48,719)	(61,447)	(78,372)	(99,496)
	438,471	553,020	705,351	895,463
CURRENT LIABILITIES	2,435,950	3,072,335	3,918,615	4,974,793
ACCOUNTS PAYABLE				
TOTAL C. LIABILITIES				
NOTES PAYABLE	730,785	921,700	117,584	1,492,438
TOTAL LIABILITIES	730,785	921,701	117,585	1,492,438
	1,461,570	1,843,401	2,351,169	2,984,876
STOCKHOLDERS' EQUITY				
CAPITAL STOCK				
RETAINED EARNINGS	600,000	600,000	600,000	600,000
	170,595	254,554	338,512	422,471
TOTAL LIABILITIES AND	974,380	1,228,934	1,567,446	1,989,917
STOCKHOLDERS' EQUITY				
	2,435,950	3,072,335	3,918,615	4,974,793

Summary of Capital Needs

In order to grow at a rate which will permit adequate control of the potential marketplace, CLI will need an additional investment of capital in the amout of $350,000 at the end of year 1. These funds will be used to finance both the promotional and advertising campaign and the investment in research and development. Both of these activities are critical to the overall success of CLI in its attempt to create a niche in the entertainment world of the home.

Forecasted balance sheets indicate that by year end of the fourth year, the capital stock will be worth $1,989,917. The fourth year also shows a net income after taxes of $1,186,132. At this point, the original investors will be in a position to make a sizeable return on their original investment. Depending upon market conditions at the time, it may be possible to expect the public market to be interested in CLI.

At this point, CLI intends to be the leader in this aspect of the entertainment world in a relatively short period of time. It is the intent of the current management to follow in the general theme of the Polaroid company in the photographic industry.

Appendix

VITA:	Dr. Alexander Lite, President
BORN:	Princeton, NY 1944
EDUCATION:	Ph.D., University of Colorado, Laser Physics M.B.A., University of Colorado, School of Business B.A., University of Denver, Engineering
EXPERIENCE:	4 years, Hewlett-Packard, Project Engineer 4 years, Hewlett-Packard, Staff Engineer 3 years, General Dynamics, Project Engineer 3 years, Spectro-Stats, Engineering-laser/fiber optics
AWARDS:	Ph.D. Award-Distinguished Thesis Fiber Association Award, Outstanding Contribution
PATENTS:	Numerous patents in the field of laser/fiber optics
PUBLICATIONS:	25 articles in the major journals in the area

Suntan, Inc.

Introduction

Begun nearly a year ago, Suntan Incorporated (SI), manufactures a line of women's bathing suit fashions which are sold to specialty boutiques in southern California. The unique characteristic of these bathing suits is that they permit the wearer to suntan while the suit is being worn. Approximately 80 percent of the sun's utraviolet rays penetrate the skin through the suits, thus allowing the individual to have an overall tan without having to expose the body to voyeurs. Strap marks and other offensive clothing marks which are the hazards of conventional bathing attire no longer result when any of the SI line of clothing is worn.

For the first year of its operation, SI has manufactured solely women's bikinis and one-piece suits. In the next year, in addition to the women's line of bathing fashions, a line of men's bathing suits will be added as well as a line of sports shirts for both men and women. In order to take advantage of the entire outdoor sports market in terms of wearing apparel, SI intends to expand into the markets where tan-through clothing is appropriate. In the third year, tennis suits and jogging pants will be added to the line. The market is endless for this type of apparel.

In order to carry out our plans in a timely manner, SI will need $450,000 in additional capital over the next year. This proposal maps the route SI intends to take in its business activities over the next two years under the assumption that additional financing is obtained. The following subjects are covered in this document:

—a brief history of the company
—a brief description of the current product and company operations
—a brief description of the management team
—a statement of objectives and goals
—a statement of the assumptions used in designing this business plan
—financial statements and projections
—a summary of the capital needs and the intended plan for using additional capital
—an appendix containing resumes of principals.

History of the Company

SI was founded one year ago by Ms. Trip with an initial capital investment of $50,000. Ms. Trip came out of the clothing industry with 20 years experience in various aspects of the industry. Having worked extensively with the major sports apparel manufacturers, Ms. Trip understands the market with which SI competes as well as the marketplace which demands the tan-through product.

While on a European vacation, Ms. Trip came across the tan-through clothing item in a Swiss biodermitological supply house. It was being used as a come-on item to the line of skin care products which the Swiss company was promoting. Upon investigating the tan-through apparel, she found that it did in fact permit the sun's rays to penetrate through the material. She discussed the idea of marketing the suits for the Swiss company in the United States; however, there appeared to be no interest on the part of the Swiss company.

Extensive research has been done regarding the product and any potential difficulties which might arise in producing it and selling it as an independent company. No regulatory problems were encountered, nor were there any proprietary difficulties with the Swiss company.

Ms. Trip then returned to the United States where she left her position with the sports apparel manufacturing firm and began work on SI. Using her contacts with the milling and designing trades, she was able to find a local fabric mill which could produce a strike-off (sample cutting) of the material she needed and in an appropriate design which was arranged through the mill's fabric print designer. From this strike-off, sales commitments were made for the two product lines—bikinis and one-piece bathing suits—which had been produced in her recently leased factory. Because bathing attire is a two-season item, the second and fourth quarters of the first year were the only ones in which production was scheduled to meet the demand at the end of the quarter. In the first year, production was contracted out to independent manufacturers who built the garments and then returned them to SI for delivery to the buyers. While this contracting arrangement was not ideal, it permitted SI to get established financially before it began its expansion phase.

In order to finance the period from production of the garments to receipt of receivables from the end buyer, factors were used. The financial details are included in the section on financing.

The Product and Operations

Tan-through material is designed much like the ordinary screen used in screen doors. The fabric is woven loosely with even spacing between the woof and warp of the fabric. Our products are made of 30 percent cotton and 70 percent polyester for durability. While the fabric appears to be see-through when held up to a light, the unique nature of our pattern design and color causes the fabric not to be see-through when worn. To allow for less tanning, we have designed our products so that varying sun penetration tolerances are available from 20 percent to 80 percent.

While at first glance it might appear that tan-through apparel is a fad item, we have found that many people prefer the overall tan, but for a number of reasons have not been able to acquire it due to the type of apparel they have been using. Tan-through clothing permits the wearer to tan and yet remain dressed.

While the production process in the first year was contracted out, SI intends to begin production on an in-house basis for the next year. The following is a brief scenario of the sales and production process:

> A freelance designer designs the bodies of the garments. A pattern maker and grader then is contracted to determine the appropriate amount of material necessary for each item. A fabric mill is located which has a competent fabric print designer. This designer then determines the appropriate colors, fabric pattern design, and fabric weave. The mill produces a strike-off of material. At the SI factory, samples of each of the products are produced and given to independent sales agents who peddle the products at the various merchandise and garment fairs and the individual stores. Upon receipt of the sales figures, production of the necessary items is begun in the SI garment factory. The items are completed and delivered to the appropriate buyer on a COD basis. All commissions are paid off at the time of delivery of the garments.

The entire production process can take from 30 to 90 days, depending upon the volume involved. Because the orders are committed before production begins, profits can be determined ahead of time on a sure basis. All potential risks for selling the garments to the retail customer are assumed by the commercial buyer.

The Management Team

The following organizational chart illustrates the proposed structure which the corporation will take upon receipt of additional capital financing.

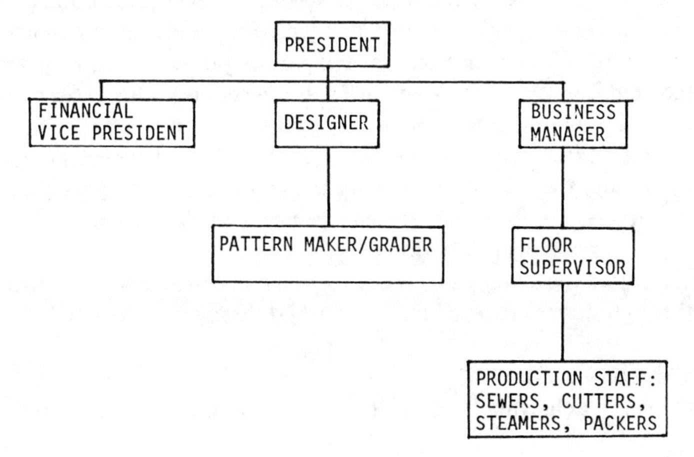

In starting this company, Ms. Trip has felt it is imperative to have competent management staff who have had experience in this garment industry. The Financial Vice President has been a part-time employee of the corporation on a consulting basis for the past year. He has experience as a controller for a similar garment manufacturing firm. Also, he has a CPA certificate.

The Business Manager is a young business school graduate with some retail experience. Primarily, he is responsible for overseeing the operations and making sure that adequate staff is maintained at all times. Also, he handles any personnel situations which might arise and can be handled at that level.

The Floor Supervisor is the head person on the production staff. She has had previous experience in the manufacturing side of the garment industry as well as formal industrial sewing training. She does all the ordering of materials/supplies which are used in the daily production process—such as thread—by placing a purchase order with the Business Manager who then arranges the necessary contracts through the Financial Vice President.

SI believes in paying competitive salaries to its employees as a means of acquiring and keeping the best available personnel. A company profit-sharing plan is being proposed. However, at this time, employees receive medical benefits, group life insurance, and a group pension plan as additional compensation. These benefits permit SI to keep competent workers and to have these workers return after periods of slow business when they are released from their employment with the company. The pension plan only applies to management (indirect labor) which is employed full-time year 'round.

During the first year of operation, the President did not draw any monies from the company as salary. The Financial Vice President was carried on the books as accounting counsel and thus was paid from G and A expenses.

Objectives and Goals

Within the next two years, SI expects to be of a substantial enough size that it will be an excellent candidate for acquisition/merger by one of the major sporting attire manufacturers. While it can continue expanding its line of tan-through attire, management feels that in the long run it will be a better candidate for one of the major garment manufacturers as a subsidiary line. While these major manufacturers have little interest in competing in the sports attire market with tan-through clothing, they would be willing to acquire a company which did market its products successfully and created its own niche. We wish to appeal to this acquisition approach over the next two years.

In order to attain the objective of being the most successful operation in this area of tan-through sports attire, SI has established three operating goals:

1. *Manufacturing Efficiency*
   Foremost in achieving success rapidly is the ability to keep costs to a

minimum. While it is important to hire the best available personnel, it also is imperative to keep miscellaneous costs to a minimum. Wherever reasonable, reworked machinery will be used rather than buying new equipment. Should newer machinery become available which would reduce the production costs dramatically, of course we will purchase it.

2. *Product Design*
   In designing our product lines and appropriate fabric design, we intend to maintain a non-faddish stance. We feel that the notion of tan-through clothing will be substantially unique enough that we need not become garish with the design. We wish to appeal to a broad market of retail buyers and therefore must create clothing which will attract the average buyer. In addition to appealing to the average buyer, we want our product lines to appeal to potential buyers of our operation. Since we would like to sell out to one of the major sports apparel companies, we want our products to be compatible with theirs.
3. *Marketing Efforts*
   The basic strategy will be to advertise our complete line of products heavily in the print media and trade journals. In the first year, we spent $50,000 on advertising which included Ms. Trip's efforts with contacts within the industry as well as trade journal literature. In the second year, we anticipate spending $200,000. We feel that it will be time to blanket the sun belt areas of the United States with articles and advertisements on our product lines. By year three, we anticipate spending $300,000 in advertising on both print media and direct mailings. Also, we intend to have some of the professional athletes sponsoring our product by wearing them during national tournaments. We will contribute to their athletic fees for this service of wearing our apparel.

In general, then, we intend to be acquired or merged within the next two years. In order to achieve that end, we have designed our three operating goals (manufacturing efficiency, product design, and marketing efforts) so that they will lead to our having an extremely profitable business in a relatively short period of time.

Assumptions of the Business Plan

The background assumptions of this business plan fall into three basic categories:

1. Financial
2. Market Analysis
3. Marketing Strategy

Financial

In developing this plan, it has been assumed that $450,000 in additional capital has been raised from an outside source. It is expected that this sum will be split between equity and convertible debentures, with the predominant amount being in debt. It is assumed also that this $450,000 will be used wisely which will result in a financially viable corporation. This money will be used to finance the change-over to in-house production of the garments as well as advertising. The financial projections shown here have assumed that the entire $450,000 was raised on an equity basis.

Market Analysis

It is difficult to estimate the size of the entire market to which sports attire is focused, much less to which tan-through sports attire might be focused. We feel that for our purposes, the market is virtually limitless. We have chosen to meet the demand in Year 1 at the 40,000 item range. At that range, we still received demand for our products, but chose to not meet that demand due to our lack of production facilities in-house. We have chosen for year 2 to meet a demand of 240,000 items. Again, demand appears to be ever-increasing; however, we felt that this was the range within which we could expand reasonably. In Year 3, we easily anticipate the demand of 720,000 items. This should be within a reasonable range for our current production facilities. Also, we would like to be acquired at some point during this Year 3 and would prefer not to have geared up our production facility to meet a greater demand.

Initially, our major competitors are manufacturers of conventional sports attire. Of course, our product line has no direct competition in the United States since we are the only ones manufacturing tan-through clothing. The European firm mentioned earlier has no intention of entering the American market. Should they decide to enter the marketplace, they would have to increase their production substantially in a brief period of time. The European garment manufacturing operation rarely is in a position to expand rapidly. This firm in particular would have to change its focus from skin care products to tan-through clothing if it intended to compete directly with us. This scenario is highly unlikely to occur.

Our American competition has little interest in competing directly at this stage of our operation. They would prefer to let us create the demand for our products and then buy us out. The major firms are of such a size at this point that they do not need nor have interest in investing their efforts in an operation such as ours. Any other potential competitors would have little difficulty in entering the marketplace once they have discovered our milling design and fabric color design; however, the potential market is large enough to accommodate several manufacturers who compete solely on style. At this point, we are unaware of any other companies producing or contemplating production of tan-through clothing.

It should be noted that the clothing industry has little room for proprietary positions unless it is in the equipment used for manufacturing of the apparel. We do not intend to compete in the equipment industry.

Marketing Strategy

We have designed the pricing structure of our products so that they are competitive with the middle range of sports attire currently being manufactured. This pricing structure permits our clothing to be compatible with conventional attire and perhaps even interchangeable in the mind of the ultimate consumer.

In addition to the competitive pricing structure, we have found from experience that we must create a market for our attire because many will think of tan-through clothing as a fad item. If we do not market carefully, we could go the way of the midi skirts of the early 70s. Our advertising will appeal both to the end buyer as well as to the retailer. We have chosen to emphasize the desirability of having a body that looks as healthy as possible. We want to capitalize upon the American vanity which sells youthfulness as an important quality. In order to combat literature which suggests that the sun's ultraviolet rays are harmful to the skin, we will suggest in our advertising that a tanning product be used over the entire body until the body has tanned. Another tactic will be to promote the purchase of several items in varying ultraviolet ray penetration strengths.

As with all clothing of this type, actual marketing to retailers is handled by independent salesmen who take an eight percent commission on average based on the discounted net sales figure. This independent salesman actually does a large proportion of the advertising when he presents the product lines to the retailers. It is worth his while, then, to sell as many of the items as possible. We feel this incentive approach is the most effective way to market our product line.

Financial Projections

Income and balance sheet statements for the first year show actual figures. The necessary capital to get the corporation going in this first year was put up by Ms. Trip in the amount of $50,000. In the first year, a small office was rented for $1,200/quarter and furnished with $5,000 worth of office equipment and furniture. A secretary/receptionist was hired to maintain the office, and a part-time business manager was employed to train in the initial phases of the business while he was completing his education. It was felt that he then would be ready to handle the office by the second year and would have been trained in our approach to managing this operation. A free-lance designer and a pattern maker/grader were hired to handle the design of the product line and the appropriate method for producing the items. As stated earlier, production was handled on a contracted basis. Net income for the year was $28,528 with stockholders' equity rising from the initial $50,000 to $78,528 by the year end. In order to finance the period from production to delivery of the product line, a factor was used which for the year cost $33,120.

Year 2 figures are projected, based upon actual sales figures of $2,134,400 in net sales for the year. Net income for the year will be $410,949 with stockholders' equity rising from $552,563 at the beginning of the year (assuming an additional $450,000 in capital) to $939,477 at year end. Advertising expenses during this year will rise to $200,000 to cover the addition of two new products to the line (men's bathing suits and sports shirts). At this point, the additional capital will be used to finance $250,000 in machinery to start in-house production and $200,000 to finance the advertising campaign. It is anticipated that the President and Financial Vice President will receive salaries totaling $55,000 for the year. The production operation will be contained in warehouse facilities as will the business office activities. The total rent will be $5,250/quarter. While overhead expenses necessarily will increase, the demand and higher production schedule will continue to permit large gross margins.

By year three, we anticipate meeting a demand of 720,000 items. Net sales for the year will be $6,844,000 with gross profit on sales of $4,250,988. Net income for the year will be $1,656,726 with stockholders' equity rising from $1,174,620 at the end of the first quarter to $2,596,203 at year end. It is at this point that we feel we will be a likely candidate for acquisition. If we are to continue to grow beyond this size, we will have to make additional investments in plant and equipment to meet the anticipated demand.

Income Statement
Year 1

	QUARTER 1	QUARTER 2	QUARTER 3	QUARTER 4	ANNUAL
NET SALES	0	184,000	0	184,000	368,000
COST OF GOODS SOLD	7,375	78,025	7,375	78,025	170,800
GROSS PROFIT ON SALES	(7,375)	105,975	(7,375)	105,975	197,200
OPERATING EXPENSES					
SELLING EXPENSES					
ADVERTISING	12,500	12,500	12,500	12,500	50,000
SALES SALARIES	0	30,912	0	30,912	87,584
OTHER	0	0	0	0	0
TOTAL	12,500	43,412	12,500	43,412	111,824
G & A EXPENSES					
ADMIN. SALARIES	0	0	0	0	0
OTHER	1,800	1,800	1,800	1,800	7,200
TOTAL	1,800	1,800	1,800	1,800	7,200
TOTAL OPERATING EXP.	14,300	45,212	14,300	43,412	119,024
INCOME FROM OPERATIONS	(21,675)	60,763	(21,675)	60,763	78,176
LESS: INTEREST EXPENSE	0	(16,560)	0	(16,560)	(33,120)
OTHER INCOME	3,000	3,000	3,000	3,000	12,000
INCOME BEFORE TAXES	(18,675)	47,203	(18,675)	47,203	57,056
INCOME TAXES	0	(14,264)	0	(14,264	(28,528)
	(18,675)	32,939	(18,675)	32,939	28,528

Balance Sheet
Year 1

	QUARTER 1	QUARTER 2	QUARTER 3	QUARTER 4
CURRENT ASSETS				
CASH/EQUIVALENTS	35,384	62,548	50,098	77,262
ACCOUNTS RECEIVABLE	0	61,334	0	61,334
TOTAL CURR. ASSETS	35,384	123,882	50,098	138,596
PLANT AND EQUIPMENT	4,275	5,050	3,825	3,600
TOTAL ASSETS	39,659	127,932	53,923	142,196
CURRENT LIABILITIES				
ACCOUNTS PAYABLE	8,334	0	8,334	0
ACCRUED FACTORY PAYROLL	0	2,334	0	2,334
INCOME TAXES PAYABLE	0	0	0	0
TOTAL C. LIABILITIES	8,334	2,334	8,334	2,334
NOTES PAYABLE	0	61,334	0	61,334
TOTAL LIABILITIES	8,334	63,668	8,334	63,668
STOCKHOLDERS' EQUITY				
CAPITAL STOCK	50,000	50,000	50,000	50,000
RETAINED EARNINGS	(18,675)	32,939	(18,576)	32,939
	31,325	64,264	45,589	78,528
TOTAL LIABILITIES STOCKHOLDERS' EQUITY	39,659	127,932	53,923	142,196

Income Statement
Projected Year 2

	QUARTER 1	QUARTER 2	QUARTER 3	QUARTER 4	ANNUAL
NET SALES	276,000	791,200	276,000	791,200	2,134,400
COST OF GOODS SOLD	142,100	301,275	142,100	301,275	886,750
GROSS PROFIT ON SALES	133,900	489,925	133,900	489,925	1,247,650
OPERATING EXPENSES					
SELLING EXPENSES					
ADVERTISING	50,000	50,000	50,000	50,000	200,000
SALES SALARIES	22,080	63,296	22,080	63,296	170,752
OTHER	0	0	0	0	0
TOTAL	72,080	113,296	72,080	113,296	370,752
G & A EXPENSES					
ADMIN. SALARIES	13,750	13,750	13,750	13,750	55,000
OTHER	3,000	3,000	3,000	3,000	12,000
TOTAL	16,750	16,750	16,750	16,750	67,000
TOTAL OPERATING EXP.	88,830	130,146	88,830	130,146	437,752
INCOME FROM OPERATIONS	45,070	359,879	45,070	359,879	809,898
LESS: INTEREST EXPENSE	0	0	0	0	0
OTHER INCOME	3,000	3,000	3,000	3,000	12,000
INCOME BEFORE TAXES	48,070	362,879	48,070	362,879	821,898
INCOME TAXES	(24,035)	(181,439)	(24,035)	(181,440)	(410,949)
NET INCOME	24,035	181,440	24,035	181,439	410,949

Balance Sheet
Projected Year 2

	QUARTER 1	QUARTER 2	QUARTER 3	QUARTER 4
CURRENT ASSETS				
CASH/EQUIVALENTS	91,573	231,392	308,998	188,616
ACCOUNTS RECEIVABLE	276,000	531,000	276,000	791,200
TOTAL CURR. ASSETS	367,573	762,392	584,998	979,816
PLANT AND EQUIPMENT	249,025	243,050	237,075	231,100
TOTAL ASSETS	616,598	1,005,442	822,073	1,210,916
CURRENT LIABILITIES				
ACCOUNTS PAYABLE	20,000	42,000	20,000	42,000
ACCRUED FACTORY PAYROLL	20,000	48,000	20,000	48,000
INCOME TAXES PAYABLE	24,035	181,439	24,035	181,439
TOTAL C. LIABILITIES	64,035	271,439	64,035	271,439
NOTES PAYABLE	0	0	0	0
TOTAL LIABILITIES	64,035	271,439	64,035	271,439
STOCKHOLDERS' EQUITY				
CAPITAL STOCK	500,000	500,000	500,000	500,000
RETAINED EARNINGS	24,035	181,440	24,035	181,439
	552,563	734,003	758,038	939,477
TOTAL LIABILITIES STOCKHOLDERS' EQUITY	616,598	1,005,442	822,073	1,210,916

Income Statement
Projected Year 3

	QUARTER 1	QUARTER 2	QUARTER 3	QUARTER 4	ANNUAL
	1,140,800	2,281,600	1,140,800	2,281,600	6,844,800
NET SALES	478,263	818,643	478,263	818,643	2,593,812
COST OF GOODS SOLD	662,537	1,462,957	662,537	1,462,957	4,250,988
GROSS PROFIT ON SALES					
OPERATING EXPENSES					
SELLING EXPENSES	75,000	75,000	75,000	75,000	300,000
ADVERTISING	91,264	182,528	91,264	182,528	547,584
SALES SALARIES	15,000	15,000	15,000	15,000	60,000
OTHER	181,264	275,528	181,264	275,528	913,584
TOTAL	14,988	14,988	14,988	14,988	59,952
G & A EXPENSES	6,000	6,000	6,000	6,000	24,000
ADMIN. SALARIES	20,988	20,988	20,988	20,988	83,952
OTHER	202,252	296,516	202,252	296,516	997,536
TOTAL					
TOTAL OPERATING EXP.					
	460,285	1,166,441	460,285	1,166,441	3,253,452
INCOME FROM OPERATIONS	0	0	0	0	0
LESS: INTEREST EXPENSE	10,000	20,000	10,000	20,000	60,000
OTHER INCOME					
	470,285	1,186,441	470,285	1,186,441	3,313,452
INCOME BEFORE TAXES					
	(235,142)	(593,219)	(235,142)	(593,219)	(1,656,726)
INCOME TAXES					
	235,143	593,220	235,143	593,220	1,656,726
NET INCOME					

Balance Sheet
Projected Year 3

	QUARTER 1	QUARTER 2	QUARTER 3	QUARTER 4
CURRENT ASSETS				
CASH/EQUIVALENTS	472,704	681,709	1,313,017	1,729,222
ACCOUNTS RECEIVABLE	855,600	1,711,200	855,600	1,711,200
TOTAL CURR. ASSETS	1,328,304	2,392,909	2,168,617	3,233,222
PLANT AND EQUIPMENT	225,125	219,150	213,175	207,200
TOTAL ASSETS	1,553,429	2,612,059	2,381,792	3,440,422
CURRENT LIABILITIES				
ACCOUNTS PAYABLE	70,667	118,000	70,667	118,000
ACCRUED FACTORY PAYROLL	73,000	133,000	73,000	133,000
INCOME TAXES PAYABLE	235,125	593,219	235,142	593,219
TOTAL C. LIABILITIES	378,809	844,219	378,809	844,219
NOTES PAYABLE	0	0	0	0
TOTAL LIABILITIES	378,809	844,219	378,809	844,219
STOCKHOLDERS' EQUITY				
CAPITAL STOCK	500,000	500,000	500,000	500,000
RETAINED EARNINGS	235,143	593,220	235,143	593,220
	1,174,620	1,767,840	2,002,983	2,596,203
TOTAL LIABILITIES STOCKHOLDERS' EQUITY	1,553,429	2,612,059	2,381,792	3,440,422

Summary of Capital Needs

In order to reach a viable size in the marketplace in a brief period of time and to be a likely candidate to conventional sports attire manufacturers for acquisition, Suntan Incorporated will need $450,000 in additional capital from an outside source. The particular arrangements concerning the financial structure of this deal are open to negotiation. We feel that the deal is attractive enough that an outside source might be interested in following our deal through to acquisition.

Forecasted balance sheets indicate that by the end of Year 3, the original capital investment of $500,000 will be worth $2,596,203. The company will be in a rapid growth stage with little competition to affect its growth. The $450,000 in outside capital will be used to purchase equipment for in-house production and for advertising in Year 2. With this additional capital, SI will be able to grow rapidly.

Depending upon the market value of the company at the end of Year 3, it is reasonable to assume that the outside investor can expect to make a sizeable return on his initial investment of $450,000 in a short period of time. This deal should be attractive to the investor who needs liquidity in a short time period.

Appendix

Ella Trip, President

Age: 38

Education: BA, MA, Rhode Island Fashion Institute of Design

Experience: 5 years retailing industry (sales/buyer, women's fashions)
5 years independent sales (women's fashions)
5 years production and administration, major apparel manufacturer

Farnie Fasceti, Financial Vice President

Age: 35

Education: BA, MBA, CPA, University of Design

Experience: 4 years major accounting firm (garment industry)
6 years major apparel manufacturing company (assistant controller/controller)

Busby Strait, Business Manager

Age: 24

Education: BS, MBA, University of Business

Experience: 4 years retailing (sales)
1 year training with Suntan Incorporated

Frank Flare, Designer

Age: 28

Education: BA, MFA, California Design Institute

Experience: 4 years retailing (sales)
2 years apprentice design
4 years freelance design (bathing suits, sports apparel for women)

Notes

Chapter 1

1. As reported in the *Small Business Investment Company Program,* Hearing before the Subcommittee on Capital Investment and Business Opportunities of the Committee on Small Businesses, House of Representatives, Washington, D.C., 1978. A study conducted by the American Electronics Association in 1978 lends credence to this argument. An analysis of the sample of 269 firms taken from the AEA membership revealed that employment growth rate in 1976 for start-up companies (less than five years old) was 115 times that for mature companies (20 years or more). The study also demonstrated that in 1976 the non-mature companies were responsible for creating an average of 89 new jobs per company, as opposed to the mature company's average of 69 new jobs.

2. All statistics referred to in the following argument are compiled from two sources: (1) *Survey of Current Business:* U.S. Department of Commerce/Bureau of Economic Analysis, April 1979, Vol. 59, No. 4; (2) *Economic Indicators,* April 1979. Joint Economic Committee by the Council of Economic Advisers. 96th Congress, 1st session.

Chapter 2

1. James Patrick Hoban, Jr., *Characteristics of Venture Capital Investments.* Ph.D. dissertation. University of Utah, 1976.

2. John B. Poindexter, *The Efficiency of Financial Markets: The Venture Capital Case.* Ph.D. dissertation. New York University, Graduate School of Business Administration, 1976.

3. William Arthur Wells, *Venture Capital Decision-Making.* Ph.D. dissertation. Carnegie-Mellon University, 1974.

4. Charles River Associates, *An Analysis of Venture Capital Market Imperfections.* Study prepared for ETIP program, National Bureau of Standards. Cambridge, 1976.

5. National Bureau of Standards ETIP program, joint project with U.S. Securities and Exchange Commission, *A Monitoring System for Effective Regulation of Venture Capital Markets.* Washington, D.C., 1977.

6. Typical of the work done by the SBA was the report entitled, *The Study of Small Business,* which was conducted and prepared by the U.S. Small Business Administration, Office of Advocacy, June 3, 1977.

7. David L. Cohen, *Small Business Capital Formation.* Prepared for the Federal Reserve Study on Capital Formation, July 1979.

8. For example:

   U.S. Congress. Joint Economic Committee, Subcommittee on Economic Growth and Stabilization. *The Costs of Government Regulation of Business.* April 10, 1978.

   U.S. House of Representatives. Committee on Small Business, Subcommittee on Capital Investment and Business Opportunities. Hearing, May 1977.

   U.S. Securities and Exchange Commission. "Examination of the Effects of Rules and Regulations on the Ability of Small Business to Raise Capital and the Impact on Small Businesses of Disclosure Requirements Under the Securities Act." Hearing. April–May 1978.

   U.S. Senate Select Committee on Small Business. Capital Formation. Hearing. February 8–10, 1978 (Part 1) and May 15, 1978 (Part 2)

9. Net Present Value Method:

$$NPV = \sum_{t=1}^{N} \frac{R_t}{(1+k)^t} - C$$

R_t = net_N cash flow
C = initial cost of the project
k = marginal cost of capital (discount rate)
N = project's expected life

$$NPV = \sum_{t=1} \frac{\alpha_t R_t}{(1+R_f)^t} - C$$

α = certainty equivalent adjustment factor
$= \frac{\text{certain return}}{\text{risky return}}$
R_f = discount rate applicable for riskless investments (such as U.S. Government Bonds)

Risk-adjusted discount rate varies the value of k based on a risk-return trade-off function (market indifference curve between risk and required rate of return).

10. Ibid., Poindexter, 1976.

Chapter 3

1. See the NVCA study, 1976.
2. The Amdahl financing was mentioned by several of the venture capitalists during the interviews as a proposal they had turned down but now wished they had financed.
3. David B. Hertz, "Risk Analysis in Capital Investments," Harvard Business Review, 42 (January-February 1964), 95–106.
4. F.M. Scherer, *Industrial Market Structure and Economic Performance.* Rand McNally and Company, Chicago, 1970.
5. Ibid., p. 4.
6. Stanley Rubel, *Guide to Venture Capital Sources.* Capital Publishing Company, Chicago, 1978.
7. Stanley Pratt, ed., "Venture Capital," Wellesley, MA.: Capitol Publishing Co.

Chapter 4

1. It should be noted that all of the following discussion is based on the researcher's translation of qualitative statements into quantitative statements. Some reduction of information naturally has taken place. In several instances, the way in which a thought was expressed and the order in which it occurred in the interview contained information which may have been valuable. It was difficult, however, to include such subtle information in the quantitative translation.

2. Many studies have produced these results. Some of the leading studies are reported in *U.S. Congress U.S. Senate Select Committee on Small Business and the House of Representatives Committee on Small Business.* Joint Hearings. August 9–10, 1978.

Chapter 5

1. Cary Alan Hoffman, *The Venture Capital Investment Process: A Particular Aspect of Regional Economic Development.* Ph.D. dissertation, The University of Texas at Austin, 1972.

Bibliography

Annotated

Charles River Associates. *An Analysis of Venture Capital Market Imperfections.* Study prepared for ETIP program, National Bureau of Standards, Cambridge, 1976.

This study of publicly-held venture capital firms and SBICs examines the structure of the venture capital industry in terms of its efficiency as a capital market.

Cohen, David C. *Small Business Capital Formation.* Study prepared for the Federal Reserve Study on Capital Formation, July 1979.

This study outlines the potential and available source of financing for small business. In addition, it covers some of the factors involved in the capital allocation process including risk, transaction costs, and government-imposed burdens on small business.

National Bureau of Standards ETIP program and U.S. Securities and Exchange Commission, joint project. *A Monitoring System for Effective Regulation of Venture Capital Markets.* Washington, D.C., 1977. The document proposes to establish one of the first government systems designed to monitor the effect of government regulations on venture capital investors.

Osborn, Richard C. "Providing Risk Capital for Small Business-Experience of the SBICs." *Quarterly Review of Economics and Business,* 1975, *15,* (1), 77–90.

This article summarizes the investments made by SBICs and illustrates with tables the categories in which these investments were made by stage of financings and size of investment.

Pratt, Stanley, ed. *Venture Capital.* Wellesley, MA: Capital Publishing Co.

This leading trade magazine of the venture capital industry provides data on both the venture capital community and their portfolio companies.

Rubel, Stanley, ed. *Guide to Venture Capital Sources.* Chicago: Capital Publishing Co., 1978.

This book is an invaluable reference. Included, in addition to a comprehensive listing of venture capital firms, is a collection of articles on how to invest and how to seek financing.

Stern, Susan. "Financing Small Business." *Small Business Reporter Series,* 1978, 13 (7). San Francisco: Bank of America.

This trade report outlines the form to be used in presenting a business plan package to an institution for consideration for funding. It also outlines sources of funding.

U.S. Congress. House. Committee on Small Business. *Future of Small Business in America.* H.R. 1810, 95th Congress, second session, 1978.

This brief report summarizes the major issues of concern to small businesses, including a discussion of the effects of economic fluctuations on small business's ability to survive.

U.S. Congress. U.S. Senate Select Committee on Small Business and the House of Representatives Committee on Small Business. *Small Business and Innovation. Joint hearings.* August 9–10, 1978.

This volume contains reprints of many technical studies on such small business issues as innovation and technology transfer, capital and credit needs, and economic costs of government regulations.

U.S. Department of Commerce. *The Role of New Technical Enterprises,* by R.S. Morse and J.O. Flender. Washington, D.C.: January 1976.
This widely-quoted report demonstrates the importance of new businesses to the economy in terms of their ability to generate jobs and tax dollars.
U.S. Small Business Administration. *Report of the SBA Task Force on Venture and Equity-Capital for Small Business.* Washington, D.C.: January 1977.
This widely-quoted report summarizes the issues venture capitalists feel are important in creating government policy. Timing of investments and dollar commitments are presented in the framework of a business's life cycle.
______. Office of Advocacy. *The Study of Small Business.* Washington, D.C.: Government Printing Office, June 3, 1977.
This report addresses in detail the concerns of small business and the impact of federal legislation on the effective operation of such businesses. Data base formation is discussed from the perspective of defining appropriate and consistent definitions of small business.

Dissertations

Hoban, James Patrick, Jr. *Characteristics of Venture Capital Investments* (Doctoral dissertation, University of Utah, 1976.) *Dissertation Abstracts International,* 1973, 37, 4469-A. (University Microfilms No. 76-30, 450.)
Hoffman, Cary Alan. *The Venture Capital Investment Process: A Particular Aspect of Regional Economic Development* (Doctoral dissertation, The University of Texas at Austin, 1972.) Dissertation Abstracts International, 1972, 33, 4641-A. (University Microfilms No. 73-7572.)
Poindexter, John B. *The Efficiency of Financial Markets: The Venture Capital Case* (Doctoral dissertation, New York University, Graduate School of Business Administration, 1976.) *Dissertation Abstracts International,* 1976, 37, 1126-A. (University Microfilms No. 76-16, 857.)
Wells, William Arthur. *Venture Capital Decision-Making* (Doctoral dissertation, Carnegie-Mellon University, 1974.) *Dissertation Abstracts International,* 1974, 35, 7475-A–7476-A. (University Microfilms No. 75-12, 505.)

Government Publications

U.S. Congress. House. Committee on Small Business. *Hearing* before the Subcommittee on Capital Investment and Business Opportunities. May 1977.
______. Joint Economic Committee. *Hearing* before The Subcommittee on Economic Growth and Stabilization. *The Costs of Government Regulations of Business.* April 10, 1978.
______. Senate. *Hearing* before The Select Committee on Small Business. *Capital Formation.* February 8–10, 1978 (Part 1) and May 15, 1978 (Part 2).
U.S. Securities and Exchange Commission. *Hearing* before the local representatives of the Commission. *Examination of the Effects of Rules and Regulations on the Ability of Small Business to Raise Capital and the Impact on Small Businesses of Disclosure Requirements Under the Securities Act.* April–May 1978.

Other

Bicksler, James L. *Methodology in Finance—Investments.* Lexington, MA: D.C. Health and Company, 1972.
Copeland, Thomas E. and Weston, J. Fred. *Financial Theory and Corporate Policy.* Reading, MA: Addison-Wesley Publishing Company, 1979.

Fienberg, Stephen E. "The Analysis of Multidimensional Contingency Tables." *Ecology,* 1970a, *51* (3), 419–433.

Friend, Irwin and Bicksler, James L., ed. *Risk and Return in Finance, Vol. 1.* Cambridge, MA: Ballinger Publishing Company, 1977.

Goodman, Leo A. "Simple Methods for Analyzing Three-Factor Interactions in Contingency Tables." *Journal of the American Statistical Association,* 1964b, *59* (306), 319–352.

______. "The Analysis of Cross-Classified Data: Independence, Quasi-Independence, and Interactions in Contingency Tables With and Without Missing Entries." *Journal of the American Statistical Association,* 1968, (324), 1091–1131.

______. "On Partitioning Chi-Square and Detecting Partial Association in Three-Way Contingency Tables." *Journal of the Royal Statistical Society.* 1969b *31B* (3), 486–498.

Hertz, David B. "Risk Analysis in Capital Investments." *Harvard Business Review,* 42 (January-February 1964), 95–106.

Kerlinger, Fred N. *Foundations of Behavioral Research.* New York: Holt, Rinehart and Winston, Inc., 1973.

Mood, Alexander M.; Graybill, Franklin A.; Boes, Duane C. *Introduction to the Theory of Statistics.* New York: McGraw-Hill Book Company, 1974.

Scherer, F.M. *Industrial Market Structure and Economic Performance.* Chicago: Rand McNally and Company, 1970.

Weston, J. Fred and Brigham, Eugene F. *Managerial Finance.* Hinsdale, IL: The Dryden Press, 1975.

Index